From
happy

Christmas 2003.

x

THE ULTIMATE
BOOK OF USELESS
INFORMATION

THE ULTIMATE BOOK OF USELESS INFORMATION

BY NOEL BOTHAM

JOHN BLAKE

Published by John Blake Publishing Ltd,
3, Bramber Court, 2 Bramber Road,
London W14 9PB, England

First published in 2003

ISBN 1 904034 76 4

British Library Cataloguing-in-Publication Data:

A catalogue record for this book is available from the British Library.

Design by ENVY

Printed in Great Britain by CPD, Wales

1 3 5 7 9 10 8 6 4 2

Papers used by John Blake Publishing are natural, recyclable products made from
wood grown in sustainable forests. The manufacturing processes conform to the
environmental regulations of the country of origin.

Every attempt has been made to contact the relevant copyright-holders, but some
were unobtainable. We would be grateful if the appropriate people could contact us.

To Lesley Lewis
with love as always

CONTENTS

SHOW
BUSINESS AND
CELEBRITIES

—— **SHOW BUSINESS AND CELEBRITIES** ——

- Bing Crosby turned down the role of Columbo in the eponymous TV detective series before Peter Falk was offered the part.

- Michael Caine fell in love with a woman he saw in a Maxwell House coffee commercial. She was Shakira Baksh, whom he later married.

- Actress Joan Collins was 50 when she posed semi-nude for *Playboy* magazine. It was a sell-out edition.

- Dean Martin, born Dino Crocetti, boxed under the name Kid Crochet as a teenager.

- Telly Savalas and Louis Armstrong died on their birthdays.

- The film version of *Oliver Twist* had its name changed to *Lost Child in Foggy City* when it was shown in China.

- Goldie Hawn was launched as an actress–comedienne after being spotted as a dancer in the chorus line on US comedy TV series *The Andy Griffith Show* in 1966.

- Tennessee Williams's real name was Thomas Lanier Williams.

—— SHOW BUSINESS AND CELEBRITIES ——

● *Wayne's World* was filmed in two weeks.

● The Marx Brothers started their show-business career as the Six Mascots, featuring brothers Leonard, Adolph, Julius, Milton, their mother Minnie and their aunt Hannah. Later the brothers changed their names to Chico, Harpo, Groucho and Gummo (in respective order).

● Maisie Wilmar-Brown, the wardrobe mistress for the Agatha Christie play *The Mousetrap*, ironed more than 36 miles (58 km) of shirts in the years between 1952 until her death in 1973.

● The first time Madonna appeared on the US *Late Show with David Letterman* her foul language had to be bleeped out twelve times. On her second appearance it only happened once.

● The term 'rock 'n' roll' was coined in 1951.

● When a reporter asked pioneer chat-show host Johnny Carson what he would like his epitaph to be, he replied, 'I'll be right back.'

● Shirley Temple was only three when she appeared in her first film, crime drama *The Red-Haired Alibi*.

—— SHOW BUSINESS AND CELEBRITIES ——

- The role that made Peter O'Toole a star, Lawrence of Arabia, had been turned down by Marlon Brando and Albert Finney.

- When Otto Preminger hired Kim Novak from Columbia Pictures for $100,000 to use her in his film *The Man with the Golden Arm*, she was still only paid $100 a week.

- Debbie Reynolds's daughter, Carrie Fisher, once said, 'I always wanted to do what my mother did. Get all dressed up – shoot people – fall in the mud. I never considered doing anything else.'

- The Bugs Bunny prototype first appeared in the cartoon *Porky's Hair Hunt* in 1938.

- The late W C Fields once said that any man who hated children and dogs couldn't be all bad. He probably turned in his grave when in 1980 his home was sold to make way for a nursery school.

- When a scene featuring Laurence Olivier was restored for the 1991 re-release of the 1960 film *Sparticus* Olivier was already dead. His voice was dubbed by Anthony Hopkins.

—— **SHOW BUSINESS AND CELEBRITIES** ——

- The BBC once rejected a claim that Chuck Berry's 1972 hit record 'Ding-a-ling' (the tale of a young man who couldn't stop playing with the song-title object and invited his friends to join in) was intended to stimulate self and mutual masturbation. Quoting Chuck Berry, they said the record was plainly about a boy who was given a bell to play with.

- As part of his fee for appearing in *Terminator 2*, Arnold Schwarzenegger, was given a Gulf Stream GIII jet aircraft.

- The blood in the famous shower scene in Alfred Hitchcock's *Psycho* was in fact Hershey's chocolate syrup.

- In the early episodes of *Star Trek* Dr McCoy's medical scanner was just an ordinary salt shaker.

- There were two *Monty Python's Flying Circus* episodes made for German and Austrian TV in 1971 and 1972. The title was *Monty Python's Fliegender Zirkus*.

- Actor John Barrymore kept a pet vulture named Maloney, which would sit on his knee and hiss.

- Irish-born Peter O'Toole claims he is never without his emerald green socks.

——SHOW BUSINESS AND CELEBRITIES——

- In pop royalty the Queen of Blues is Dinah Washington, the Queen of Soul is Aretha Franklin, the Queen of Disco is Donna Summer, the King of Swing is Benny Goodman, the King of the Cowboys is Roy Rogers and the King is Elvis Presley.

- Errol Flynn once won $30,000 answering questions on sailing on the 1950s television quiz show *The Big Surprise*.

- Silent-movie star Ben Turpin had a $100,000 insurance policy against his trademark crossed eyes ever straightening out.

- In *The Adventures of Robin Hood* Olivia de Havilland rode the horse that later found fame as famous cowboy steed Trigger. It was before Roy Rogers rode him to movie stardom and changed his name from the then Golden Cloud.

- Superman appears in every episode of the US TV series *Seinfeld*. There is a model figure of the superhero on a shelf in Jerry Seinfeld's apartment.

- The most expensive silent movie ever made was the 1926 epic *Ben Hur*, which cost $3.9 million.

—— SHOW BUSINESS AND CELEBRITIES ——

- Peter Ustinov was signed for the part of Inspector Jacques Clousseau but pulled out at the last moment, opening the way for Peter Sellers to play the part.

- David Selznick, producer of *Gone With the Wind*, was fined $5,000 by the Motion Picture Association of America for letting the word 'damn' be used.

- The legs shown walking down the street in the opening of *Saturday Night Fever* were not John Travolta's but those of his stand-in, Jeff Zinn.

- Samuel Goldwyn's real name was Samuel Goldfish.

- Burt Reynolds now lives in the Florida holiday home of Chicago gangster Al Capone.

- Don McLean's famous song was inspired by the name of the plane in which Buddy Holly died – American Pie.

- Anthony Quinn got his first film part in *The Plainsman* (1937) by pretending to be a Cheyenne Indian.

- Sylvia Miles had the shortest performance ever nominated for an Oscar in the film *Midnight Cowboy*. Her entire role lasted only six minutes.

—— SHOW BUSINESS AND CELEBRITIES ——

- Before he became a comedian Bob Hope was a boxer known as Packy East.

- As a young actor James Dean earned food money testing stunts for the TV game *Beat the Clock*.

- The first custard pie ever thrown on screen was in the 1950s silent comedy *Keystone Kops*. Mabel Normand threw a pie at Ben Turpin.

- The first British sound movie was Alfred Hitchcock's 1929 *Blackmail*.

- The first name of TV detective Lieutenant Columbo was Phillip.

- The real name of the Looney Tunes music is 'The Merry-go-round is Broken Down'.

- Doris Day turned down the role of Mrs Robinson in *The Graduate* in 1967 because she said she could not picture herself making love on a film set. Anne Bancroft was given the role and was hugely successful.

- White-out was invented by the mother of Mike Nesmith of the Monkees.

—— SHOW BUSINESS AND CELEBRITIES ——

- Paul McCartney's mother was a midwife.

- Al Capone was so pleased with the 1932 film *Scarface* he gave director Howard Hawkes a miniature machine gun as a thank-you present.

- Telly Savalas first shaved his head not for the role of Kojak but for the part of Pontius Pilate in *The Greatest Story Ever Told*.

- Cuban dictator Fidel Castro gave his first TV interview after seizing power from Ed Murrow. Castro appeared wearing only his pyjamas.

- W C Fields's full name was William Claude Dukenfield.

- After turning down the role of Marshall Matt Dylan in the TV show *Gunsmoke,* John Wayne recommended his good friend, James Arness, for the part. It made him a top star.

- To open their first ever theatre in 1903 in New Castle, Pennsylvania, Warner Brothers Jack, Harry, Sam and Albert borrowed the 99 chairs they needed from the local undertaker. They had to be taken back for funerals.

—— SHOW BUSINESS AND CELEBRITIES ——

- Tom Selleck, who played heart-throb Thomas Magnum in the TV series *Magnum, PI*, was not chosen by the girl when he appeared as a contestant on *The Dating Game*.

- Shirley Temple always had 56 curls in her hair.

- The first video ever played on MTV Europe was 'Money for Nothing' by Dire Straits.

- Sam Goldwyn spent an extra $20,000 reshooting a scene in *Bulldog Drummond* because he didn't understand the word 'din'. He had the word 'noise' substituted.

- Spencer Tracy said he would only take the part of the Penguin in the *Batman* TV series if he was allowed to kill Batman.

- Actors Studio legend Lee Strasberg said his two students who stood out way above the rest were Marilyn Monroe and Marlon Brando.

- Johnny Mathis dubbed Miss Piggy's singing voice in *The Muppet Movie* (1979).

- In film-editing lingo R2 D2 – the robot in *Star Wars* – means Reel 2, Dialogue 2.

—— SHOW BUSINESS AND CELEBRITIES ——

- US Senator Barry Goldwater attended the opening-night ceremonies and festivities at Bugsy Siegel's famous Las Vegas casino. He was hopping mad when they left him out of the movie *Bugsy*.

- Margaret Rutherford's stage debut at the age of 33 was as a long-nosed fairy in a pantomime called *Little Jack Horner*.

- The longest list of film credits on record before *The Matrix Reloaded* was for the 1988 film *Who Framed Roger Rabbit?*. There were 763 names. It might have been 764 but Kathleen Turner, who dubbed the voice of Jessica Rabbit, asked not to be included in the credits.

- Winston Churchill was the only person to appear smoking a cigar on the early TV news show *The Camel News Caravan*, sponsored by Camel Cigarettes.

- Only one woman, Tracy Reed, appeared in Stanley Kubrick's *Dr Strangelove, or How I Learned to Stop Worrying and Love the Bomb*.

- Elton John's uncle was a professional soccer player. He broke his leg while playing for Nottingham Forest in the 1959 FA Cup Final.

—— SHOW BUSINESS AND CELEBRITIES ——

- The snow scenes in the film *It's a Wonderful Life* were shot during a record heatwave in Southern California.

- The part of outlaw Jesse James has been played by many great Hollywood stars, but the first actor ever to play the role on screen was James's own son, Jesse James Jr, in the 1921 silent movie *Under the Black Flag*.

- Catherine Deneuve had a son by Roger Vadim and a daughter by Marcello Mastroianni but was married to neither.

- In all his film contracts James Stewart was granted the right to select all the hats he would wear on screen.

- Actor David Niven made his screen debut as a Mexican, wearing a blanket, in the very first *Hopalong Cassidy* movie.

- The only cast member of the movie *M*A*S*H* to appear as a regular in the television series was Gary Burghoff, who played Corporal Radar O'Reilly in both.

- In *Arsenic and Old Lace* staring Cary Grant, a tombstone shown in the film is inscribed with Grant's real name, Archibald Leach.

── SHOW BUSINESS AND CELEBRITIES ──

- Artists had to draw 6,469,952 spots for the 1961 Walt Disney cartoon film *One Hundred and One Dalmatians.*

- James Stewart played the accordion in a tea room before being offered his first part in a Broadway play. He showed off his little-known skill in the 1955 film *The Man from Laramie.*

- Michael Jackson owns the rights to the South Carolina State anthem.

- The cancan was derived from the French word for 'scandal' and became popular in the 1830s. Girls lifting their skirts and showing their legs, stockings and underwear took Paris by storm.

- When Katherine Hepburn was a child she shaved her head, wore trousers and called herself Jimmy because she so wanted to be a boy.

- Boris Karloff's real name was William Henry Pratt and he was educated at Dulwich College, England.

- Sean Connery has to have the tattoos on his arm covered by make-up when filming. The tattoos declare his love for his mum and dad, and for Scotland.

—— SHOW BUSINESS AND CELEBRITIES ——

- MGM's first picture with sound, the 1928 *White Shadows in the South Seas* had only one word of dialogue: 'Hello'.

- Richard Gere's middle name is Tiffany.

- Fred Astaire had his legs insured for a mere £53,000 while his dancing partner, Cyd Charise, had hers covered for £3.5 million.

- Simon Templar was dubbed 'the Saint' because of his initials 'ST'.

- Margaret Hamilton, the Wicked Witch of the West in *Wizard of Oz*, was once a kindergarten teacher.

- Gary Cooper believed *Gone with the Wind* would be 'the biggest flop in Hollywood's history' and turned down the leading role as Rhett Butler.

- When President Ronald Reagan began using the term 'Star Wars' to describe his computer-controlled space defence system George Lucas launched a lawsuit against him to protect his film title.

- When Bugs Bunny made his first appearance in 1935 he was called Happy Rabbit.

—— SHOW BUSINESS AND CELEBRITIES ——

- When in 1986 Joan Rivers appeared on national TV with Victoria Principal, with whom she had a long-standing feud, the comedienne deliberately gave out the actress's unpublished home telephone number.

- More extras were used in the 1981 film *Gandhi* than in any other movie; 300,000 were used for only a ten-minute funeral sequence.

- Despite being offered $4 million each, Paul Newman, Robert Redford and Steve McQueen all turned down the role of Superman. It eventually went to Christopher Reeve who was paid $250,000.

- The first TV sitcom couple to share a double bed were the Munsters Lily and Herman during the 1964/5 season.

- Charlie Chaplin died on Christmas Day 1977.

- In her first television appearance in 1954, Lauren Bacall recited the poem *Casey at the Bat*.

- After Harrison Ford's brief 1966 appearance as a bellboy in *Dead Heat on a Merry-go-round* he was told, 'Kid, you ain't got it.'

—— SHOW BUSINESS AND CELEBRITIES ——

- Sean Connery once worked as a coffin polisher.

- The race around the Great Court at Trinity College, Cambridge, featured in the 1981 film *Chariots of Fire* was actually filmed at Eton College because the Trinity dons refused to acknowledge the movie in any way.

- *The Flintstones* lawyer who never lost a case was called Perry Masonry.

- The original title of the television series *Charlie's Angels* was *The Alley Cats.*

- Lucille Ball did not become a redhead until the age of 30 – after twelve years as a platinum blonde and eighteen years as a natural brunette.

- Leonard Skinner was the name of the gym teacher of the boys who went on to form Lynyrd Skynyrd. He once told them: 'You boys will never amount to nothing.' The band's front man, Ronnie Van Zant, decided to adopt the name but change the spelling, as a joke on his former teacher.

- Film star Sean Connery represented Scotland in the 1952 Mr Universe contest.

—— SHOW BUSINESS AND CELEBRITIES ——

- The music group Simply Red is named because of their love for Manchester United football team, which has a red home strip.

- Lucille Ball was thrown out of the New York Robert Minton–John Murray Anderson School of Drama at the age of fifteen because her instructor thought she was 'too quiet and shy'.

- In a two-hour movie there are 10,800 ft (3,292 m) of film.

- Roger Moore has it written into all his film contracts that he must be provided with an unlimited supply of hand-rolled Cuban cigars during filming.

- When Tom and Jerry made their debut in the 1940 cartoon *Puss Gets the Boot*, Tom was called Jasper and Jerry didn't have a name at all.

- In *Psycho* the colour of Mrs Bates's dress is periwinkle blue.

- Marilyn Monroe's last ever line in a film was 'How do you find your way back in the dark?' spoken to Clark Gable in *The Misfits*.

──SHOW BUSINESS AND CELEBRITIES──

- Mel Blanc, the voice of Bugs Bunny, was allergic to carrots.

- Keith Moon of The Who inspired the Muppet drummer Animal.

- The Captain of the USS Enterprise in *Star Trek*, before James T Kirk ever came on board, was Captain Christopher Pike.

- The full name of the Fonz, played by Henry Winkler in the TV series *Happy Days*, was Arthur Herbert Fonzarelli.

- The man who became President of Kenya, Jomo Kenyatta, played a tribal chief in the 1935 British film *Sanders of the River.*

- A real cruise liner, the *Isle de France*, was deliberately sunk to provide the dramatic climax to the film *The Last Voyage* in 1960.

- There are 1,943 names listed in the closing credits of *The Matrix Reloaded.*

- Aerosmith's 'Dude Looks Like a Lady' was written about Vince Neil of Motley Crew.

—— SHOW BUSINESS AND CELEBRITIES ——

● Oprah Winfrey's first name should have been the biblical name Orpah, from the Book of Ruth, except the midwife made a mistake in spelling it when she filled out the birth certificate.

● Boris Karloff's first film role was as a $5-a-day extra (a Mexican soldier) in a non-horror silent movie, *His Majesty the American* (1919).

● Ronald Reagan and his second wife, Nancy Davis, appeared opposite each other in the movie *Hellcats of the Navy*.

● Half the world's population has seen at least one James Bond movie.

● *The Muppet Show* was banned from television in Saudi Arabia because one of its stars was Miss Piggy. Pigs are forbidden to Muslims.

● According to Warner Brothers, Sam Peckinpah used more ammunition – 90,000 blank rounds – than the entire Mexican Revolution when he made *The Wild Bunch*.

● In the original draft for *Star Trek* the name of the USS Enterprise was down as the USS Yorktowne.

—— SHOW BUSINESS AND CELEBRITIES ——

- The real Butch Cassidy did not die in Bolivia but returned home, minus the Sundance Kid, and became an adding-machine manufacturer.

- Howard Taylor (brother of Elizabeth) was so determined not to take a screen test arranged by his pushy, stage-struck mother that he shaved his head the night before.

- All characters in *The Flintstones* had four fingers on each hand and three toes on each foot.

- Singer Bob Dylan appeared in the 1973 film *Pat Garrett and Billy the Kid* as a character named Alias.

- Walt Disney had wooden teeth.

- Actress Farrah Fawcett had a tap named after her – the gold-plated Farrah Faucet.

- Caesar and Cleo were the early stage names of Sonny and Cher Bono.

- Charles Bronson and James Coburn both turned down the part of the Man With No Name in the spaghetti western *A Fistful of Dollars* before Clint Eastwood was signed for the role.

—— SHOW BUSINESS AND CELEBRITIES ——

- Orson Welles was only 25 years old when he co-wrote, produced, directed and starred in the 1941 masterpiece *Citizen Kane*.

- Pia Zadora's first movie role was as a young child protagonist in *Santa Claus Conquers the Martians*.

- The phrase 'cameo role' was invented by Mike Todd when he made *Around the World in Eighty Days* in 1955. He had a host of top Hollywood stars playing bit parts.

- Bob Dylan's real name is Robert Zimmerman.

- Alan Ladd had a hot-dog stall known as 'Tiny's' – he was only 5ft 6 in tall – before breaking into films.

- Debra Winger was the voice of ET.

- The calabash pipe, most often associated with Sherlock Holmes, was not used to portray him until William Gillette (an American) played him on stage. Gillette needed a pipe he could keep in his mouth while he spoke his lines.

- Jean Harlow was the first actress to appear on the cover of *Life* magazine.

—— **SHOW BUSINESS AND CELEBRITIES** ——

- Indiana Jones's first name was Henry.

- Leonard Nimoy, who went on to play Mr Spock in *Star Trek*, first appeared in alien guise in the pilot of a TV science-fiction series, *The Zombie Vanguard*. He played a Martian in the zombie army.

- Spot, Mr Data's cat in *Star Trek: The Next Generation*, was played by six different cats.

- Rita Hayworth's real name was Margarita Cansino.

- Woody Allen's legal name is Heywood Allen, but his real name was originally Allen Stewart Konigsberg.

- Arnold Schwarzenegger made his screen debut as Arnold Strong in the 1970 Italian TV film *Hercules in New York*.

- The roaring lion in the MGM logo was named Volney and lived in Memphis Zoo.

- Gene Autry was the only entertainer to have all five stars on Hollywood's Walk of Fame – that is, one for each of the five categories of film, TV, recording, radio and theatre.

—— SHOW BUSINESS AND CELEBRITIES ——

- The Beatles song 'Martha My Dear' was written by Paul McCartney about his sheepdog.

- In 1983 a Japanese artist made a perfect copy of the *Mona Lisa* out of toast.

- Dan Ackroyd's conehead from US sketch comedy show *Saturday Night Live* was auctioned off at £1,500.

- The name of the ship in which Dr Doolittle sailed in the 1967 film was *The Flounder.*

- John Wayne began his film career in a series of western movies as Singin' Sam, the silver screen's first singing cowboy. Unfortunately he couldn't make records because his singing voice and guitar playing were both dubbed.

- The 19-ft-long Batmobile used in the TV series *Batman*, starring Adam West, covered only four miles to the gallon.

- 'Mr Mojo Risin' is an anagram of Jim Morrison.

- Elton John's real name is Reginald Dwight. 'Elton' came from Elton Dean, a Bluesology sax player, and 'John' came from Long John Baldry, founder of Blues Inc.

—— SHOW BUSINESS AND CELEBRITIES ——

- In 1976 Sarah Caldwell became the first woman to conduct the Metropolitan Opera in New York City.

- Hulk Hogan's real name is Terry Bolle.

- Because D W Griffith wanted one of his stars in the 1916 silent film *Intolerance* to have eyelashes that brushed her cheeks, false eyelashes were invented.

- Three thousand rats were specially bred for the film *Indiana Jones and the Last Crusade*.

- In the movie *The Right Stuff* there is a scene where a government recruiter for the Mercury Astronaut Programme, played by Jeff Goldblum, is in a bar at Muroc Dry Lake, California. His partner suggests legendary jet test pilot Chuck Yeager as a good astronaut candidate. Goldblum proceeds to bad-mouth Yeager, claiming they need someone who went to college. During this conversation the real Chuck Yeager is playing the bartender, who is standing behind the recruiters and eavesdropping. General Yeager is listed low in the movie's credits as 'Fred'.

- The licence plate of the General Lee in *The Dukes of Hazzard* is CNH 320.

—— SHOW BUSINESS AND CELEBRITIES ——

- Sylvester Stallone worked as a sweeper of the lion cages in New York's Central Park Zoo to pay his way while trying to break into acting.

- The first film to be released in CinemaScope in 1953 was *The Robe*.

- Bert's goldfish in the TV series *Sesame Street* were named Lyle and Talbot, after the actor Lyle Talbot.

- Popeye's girlfriend, Olive Oil, wore a size 14A shoe.

- The only X-rated film to win an Oscar for Best Picture was *Midnight Cowboy*. It was later reduced to an R rating.

- The initial 'T' in *Star Trek* Captain James T Kirk's name stands for Tiberius.

- Under the Motion Picture censorship code, which was effective from 1934 to 1968, a screen kiss could only last 30 seconds before being labelled 'indecent'.

- The word 'pregnant' was banned by censors from the script of TV sitcom *I Love Lucy* in 1952 – even though Lucy was obviously expecting and her son's birth was a major feature in that season's episodes.

—— SHOW BUSINESS AND CELEBRITIES ——

- Ian Anderson, not Jethro Tull, is the name of the rock singer responsible for such songs as 'Aqualung' and 'Thick as a Brick'. Jethro Tull is the name of the band. And the original Jethro Tull was an English horticulturist who invented the seed drill.

- Mia Farrow once gave her vital statistics as 20–20–20.

- The longest ever sword fight on film, lasting six and a half minutes, was between Stewart Granger and Mel Ferrer in the 1952 film *Scaramouche*.

- James Doohan, who plays Lieutenant Commander Montgomery Scott in *Star Trek*, is missing the entire middle finger of his right hand.

- Colonel Sherman Potter's horse in the TV series *M*A*S*H* was called Sophie.

- Rudolph Nureyev once danced a *pas de deux* from *Swan Lake* with Miss Piggy on *The Muppet Show*.

- *The Cotton Club* was involved in so many lawsuits before its release in 1984 that the director included the name of the winning lawyers on the closing credits.

—— SHOW BUSINESS AND CELEBRITIES ——

- The actor who played the T-1000 in *Terminator 2*, Robert Patrick, is the brother of the lead singer with Filter.

- Marlon Brando, Mel Gibson, Clark Gable and Errol Flynn have all played Fletcher Christian in *Mutiny on the Bounty*.

ROYALS

ROYALS

- In her sixties, Queen Elizabeth I often sat in front of her whole court with her dress thrown open at the front to expose her breasts. No reason was ever given for this amazing royal display.

- In his personal prayer book King George III struck out the words 'our most religious and gracious king' and substituted 'a most miserable sinner'.

- Within minutes of delivering a speech on road safety, in 1957, Prince Philip crashed his car.

- According to the bible King Solomon had 700 wives.

- The Queen always writes with a fountain pen which belonged to her father, King George VI.

- It is a popular misconception that the royal family cannot vote in political elections. It is only the Queen, herself, who is not allowed to vote. Other members of the family merely chose not to.

- An aide announced Napoleon's death to King George IV in 1821 with the words: 'Your greatest enemy is dead, sir.' The king replied: 'By God, is she?' Believing his aid was referring to the queen.

ROYALS

- Prince Philip keeps a collection of press cartoons of himself on the walls of his lavatory in Sandringham.

- Prince Charles's first Shetland pony was called Fum.

- Prince Charles used the pick-up line on girls, 'I like to give myself heirs' when he attended Cambridge University. Prince William's pick up line at St Andrew's University is 'I'm the next king. Wanna pull?'

- US President Richard Nixon tried to marry off the then, 23 year old, Prince Charles, to his daughter Tricia. Nixon and his wife even going to the extent of deliberately leaving the couple alone in rooms in the White House, so they could get 'better acquainted'.

- In official photographs for their wedding stamps Prince Charles stood on a soapbox to give the impression he was much taller than Diana. For their engagement pictures, on stairs, she was made to stand on a lower step.

- Queen Mary turned up at a 1938 Buckingham Palace party wearing five diamond necklaces at one and the same time.

- Eton College was founded by King Henry VI in 1440.

ROYALS

- After they had run a series of revealing palace stories Prince Philip described the *Daily Express* as 'a bloody awful newspaper. It is full of lies, scandal and imagination. It is a vicious newspaper.'

- King George V described his ancestors, buried in St George's Chapel, Windsor, as 'a strange busload to be travelling through eternity together.'

- Prince Charles would sometimes adopt the name Charlie Chester when signing himself into clubs.

- The Queen's nickname for her grandfather, King George VI was 'Grandpapa England'.

- Queen Victoria adopted the nickname Pussy, for her eldest daughter, the Princess Royal.

- In the 17th Century, King Charles II twice won the horse race, the Newmarket Cup, riding his own horse.

- All royal babies are baptised with water brought from the River Jordan.

- Henry II's second wife Eleanor was 40 when their first child was born.

ROYALS

- King Charles II's coronation was delayed because there was no regalia. Oliver Cromwell had sold it all and it had to be replaced.

- The heart of King Henry VIII's beheaded wife Anne Boleyn was buried separately from her body in a church in Suffolk.

- George VI, George V, Charles I and Henry VIII were all second sons who succeeded to the throne.

- Clive Jenkins once said of Prince Philip: 'He's the best argument for republicanism since George III.'

- The British monarch with the largest number of illegitimate children was King Henry I with 21. King Charles II was a worthy runner up with 15.

- There were 130 ships in the Spanish Armada which was sent to conquer England in 1586 by Spain's King Philip II.

- Nell Gwynne, always referred to her lover King Charles II as Charles the third. Her previous two lovers had also been called Charles.

- Prince Philip wears contact lenses.

ROYALS

- Queen Victoria often put on a Scottish accent when travelling north of the border.

- King George V banned his son, King Edward VIII, for a year from playing billiards, after he miscued and slit the cloth on the table.

- Princess Margaret was afraid of the dark.

- Prince Andrew refused to wear shorts under his kilt as a child to be like Prince Philip. 'Papa doesn't wear anything and neither shall I!' He would cry.

- Princess Diana was the first royal bride not to use the word 'obey' in her marriage vows.

- Queen Victoria described votes for women as 'a mad, wicked folly.'

- Discussing public duty Princess Anne said, 'There is a limit to how interesting a forty acre field can be, in my opinion.'

- The Queen's description of Niagara Falls: 'It looks very damp.'

- Princess Diana was a very enthusiastic tap dancer.

ROYALS

- The Queen Mother could play the bongo drums expertly.

- The sirloin was introduced when King James I knighted a joint of beef (a loin), which was particularly tasty.

- Queen Victoria was taught to sing by the composer Mendelssohn.

- King Edward VIII was an accomplished banjo player. He could also play the ukulele and once composed and played a tune on the bagpipes.

- The Queen and Prince Philip are third cousins through their descent from Queen Victoria and are also related through King George III and King Christian IX of Denmark.

- Anne of Cleves was so different to the portraits of her he had been shown, that King Henry VIII asked courtiers: 'Have you brought me the Flanders mare?'

- King Edward I was forty years older than his second wife, Margaret.

- King James I joined his friend Philip Herbert and his bride in bed on their honeymoon night!

ROYALS

- Princess Augusta of Saxe-Gotha was physically sick during her wedding to Frederick, Prince of Wales in 1736.

- Queen Victoria told her eldest daughter, when she became pregnant, 'It really is too dreadful to have the first year of one's married life and happiness spoilt by discomfort and misery – I was furious at being in that position.'

- Henry VIII's longest marriage was to Catherine of Aragon, his first bride. It lasted 23 years and 11 months. His shortest was to Anne of Cleves. The marriage ended in divorce after 6 months.

- The Queen was born on a Wednesday.

- King George I of Greece used the huge ballroom of his Athens palace as a roller skating ring.

- Birdcage Walk is thus called because King Charles II kept his aviary there in St James's Park.

- The English Queen with the most Christian names was Mary, wife of King George V who had eight. Victoria Mary Augusta Louisa Olga Pauline Claudine Agnes.

ROYALS

- The Queen Mother used to describe her clothes as 'my props'.

- When they made Prince Charles an honorary chieftain the Kainai tribe of Alberta, Canada, gave him the name of Prince Red Chow.

- Prince Andrew was nicknamed *the sniggerer* by his schoolmates at Gordonstoun. At the same school Prince Edward was nicknamed *Jaws* because of the metal braces on his teeth.

- At Timbertops school in Australia Prince Charles was nicknamed 'Pommy Bastard'.

- Prince Charles was named *Hooligan of the Year* in 1978 by the RSPCA after he had hunted boar in Liechtenstein.

- Queen Victoria refused to believe in the existence of lesbianism and scratched out all reference to sex between women in the anti homosexuality bill before she signed it. That is why female homosexuality was never prosecuted in Britain.

- The Theatre Royal in Drury Lane was founded by King Charles II in 1663.

ROYALS

- King Edward V reigned only three months in 1483 before being deposed. He was never crowned. His descendant, King Edward VIII was also never crowned. He abdicated before his coronation had been due to take place.

- The longest British reign was that of Queen Victoria who was on the throne 63 years and 7 months from 1837 to 1901.

- The shortest reign was that of Lady Jane Grey which lasted only nine days in 1553. She was only 16 when she was beheaded.

- Queen Victoria's funeral was the first royal funeral to be held during the day and the first to involve pageantry. Previous royal funerals had taken place at night and were strictly private affairs.

- Princes William and Harry are uncircumcised.

- In the past millenium there have been three occasions when three kings ruled in a single year – 1066 (Edward the Confessor, King Harold and King William the Conqueror), 1483 (Edward IV, Edward V and Richard III) and 1936 (George V, Edward VIII and George VI).

ROYALS

- King William IV of England was also King William III of Scotland, William II of Ireland and King William I of Hanover.

- King Charles I favourite joke was to place his court dwarf, 18 inches tall Jeffrey Hudson, between two halves of a loaf and pretend to eat him.

- It is said that King James I became a lifelong heavy drinker because his wet nurse was an alcoholic and he received such copious quantities of the hard stuff through her milk.

- King Edward III died of gonorrhea, which he caught from his mistress when he was 65 years of age.

- Henry VIII and Edward VI also died of venereal disease. George IV and William IV both died of cirrhosis of the liver.

- After meeting the Duke of Kent jazz musician, Louis Armstrong, sent him a 21st birthday message in which he wrote 'To Black Jack, the sharpest little cat I know. Satch.'

- The Queen Mother's favourite television show was *Dad's Army*

ROYALS

- The Duchess of Wurttemberg had her spectacles accidentally knocked off during the wedding banquet for Prince Philip's parents. When she lashed out with her handbag in furious retaliation she hit the wrong person over the head. She couldn't see.

- In Balmoral Princess Margaret dressed up as Last of the Red Hot Mamas, Sophie Tucker to give a full, birthday party impersonation.

- Not a lover of the arts, King George II would frequently scream in his thickly accented English: 'No more bainting, blays or boetry.'

- King Richard II invented the handkerchief.

- King Edward VII's favourite dog, Ceasar, had 'I am Ceasar – the King's Dog' on his collar.

- Queen Elizabeth I banned all mirrors from the royal apartments during the last decade of her life.

- Princess Anne told an American press conference in 1975: 'Everything I've seen written thus far is a copy of every falsification I've ever seen written about me. Even the pictures are not of me.'

ROYALS

- Even when they dined alone, with no extra guests, King George V insisted on his sons wearing full evening dress – white tie, tails and decorations, including the garter star and sash.

- Six of Britain's kings were homosexuals. They were William II, Richard I, Edward II, Richard II, James I and William III.

- Prince Philip once remarked, 'Constitutionally, I don't exist.'

- When Prince Philip gave away Hèléne Cordet, the television personality, at her wedding, and became godfather to both her children – it not surprisingly raised suggestions that they were his own.

- Prime Minister Gladstone said of King Edward VII: 'He knows everything except what is in books.'

- Prince Charles twice failed his Maths 'O' Level.

- William of Orange was 4 inches smaller than his wife, Queen Mary.

- Princess Anne once said she would like to have been a long distance lorry driver.

ROYALS

- The Queen named one of her horses 'Charlton' after brothers Bobby and Jackie who helped lead England to victory in the 1966 World Cup.

- The Queen's racing colours are red and blue.

- In dire financial straits, when a teenager, the Queen Mother sent her father a telegram message reading 'S.O.S., L.S.D., R.S.V.P.'

- The Queen Mother suffered from whooping cough on her honeymoon.

- Anne Boleyn had three breasts and an extra finger.

- King Edward VII had an American bowling alley installed at Sandringham.

- The last time the Queen curtsied was in 1952 – to her father's body in St George's Chapel, Windsor.

- As a prince, King Edward VI had a 'whipping boy' named Barnaby Fitzpatrick, who was beaten every time the prince misbehaved during lessons.

- Queen Elizabeth I had over 2000 dresses.

ROYALS

- The Bishop of London had one of his own, sound, teeth extracted to show Queen Elizabeth I how easily one of her own, rotten, teeth could be removed.

- Prince Philip quit smoking on the night before his wedding.

- *The Times* obituary on King George IV reported, 'There never was an individual less regretted by his fellow creatures than this deceased king.'

- After the Duke died the Duchess of Windsor always kept a loaded pistol by her bedside.

- There is a secret station, on the London Underground system beneath Buckingham Palace, so that the family can escape to Heathrow Airport in an emergency.

- To prevent her secrets being revealed to snoopers the Queen always uses black blotting paper

- Queen Victoria was the first woman to use chloroform during childbirth.

- Richard II once had to pawn his crown because he was such a spendthrift.

ROYALS

- The Queen has a special car mascot – a silver model of St George and the Dragon – which is transferred to any royal car in which she is travelling.

- King George IV's nickname for his much unloved wife, Queen Caroline, was *The Fiend*.

- The Queen is an excellent mimic and sometimes entertains the family aping the Prime Ministers she has known in the last half century.

- The last widowed queen of England to remarry was Queen Catherine Parr, who married Lord Seymoor in 1547 – her fourth husband.

- So anxious was he not to shiver with cold in case people thought him to be trembling with fear that King Charles I wore two shirts for his execution.

- Sometimes Prince Philip hides a radio in his top hat when he attends the Ascot races – because he hates racing and prefers to listen to the cricket.

- When Lord Harris first turned up at Ascot wearing his, now famous, trade mark tweed, King Edward VII greeted him with the words: 'Mornin' Harris going rattin'?'

--- **ROYALS** ---

- The Queen has ten residences available to her if necessary. Buckingham Palace, Windsor Castle, St James's Palace, Kensington Palace, Hampton Court palace, Balmoral, Sandringham, Holyrood House, the Tower of London and the Palace of Westminster – which is still one of the monarch's official residences.

SCIENCE AND
NATURE

SCIENCE AND NATURE

- A bird has to fly at a minimum speed of 11 mph (18 kph) to be able to keep itself aloft.

- The British Goat Society was formed in 1879.

- The Arctic tern enjoys more daylight hours than any other living creature. Each year it spends four months of constant daylight in the Arctic before swimming south to spend four months of constant daylight in the Antarctic. It makes the 20,000-mile (32-km) return trip every year.

- Americans use 16,000 tons (16,256 tonnes) of aspirin each year.

- Only 25% of babies are born on the day predicted by the doctor or midwife.

- Dogs can suffer from tonsillitis but not appendicitis as they don't have an appendix.

- Banging your head against a wall uses 150 calories an hour.

- The average caterpillar has 248 muscles in its head.

- The dumbest dogs in the world are Afghan hounds.

SCIENCE AND NATURE

- The May fly lives only six hours, but its eggs take three years to hatch.

- The word 'byte' is a contraction of 'by eight'.

- The first hard drive available for the Apple computer had a capacity of 5 Mb.

- Intelligent people have more zinc and copper in their hair.

- Only two animal species wage war on their own kind – ants and humans.

- The sloth can starve to death even with a plentiful supply of food if there are too many cloudy days in a row. It needs sunshine to raise its body temperature so that the bacteria in its stomach are warm enough to digest the food it eats. It can take up to four days to digest even a single stomachful of food.

- The housefly hums in the middle octave of the key of F.

- Crocodiles cannot stick their tongues out.

- On average there are seven to nine peas in a pod.

--------- **SCIENCE AND NATURE** ---------

- A snail can sleep for three years.

- The eyes of some birds weigh more than their brains.

- One year contains 31,557,600 seconds.

- There are at least 100,000 chemical reactions going on in a normal human brain every second.

- City dogs live about three years longer than country dogs.

- A Laforte fracture is a fracture of all facial bones.

- An infinity sign is called a lemniscate.

- During pregnancy a woman's blood volume can increase by up to 50% to a total of twelve pints. This is in reserve against possible loss of blood during delivery.

- Vets at London Zoo once fitted a snake with a glass eye.

- A computer program named HITMAN (Homicide Information Tracking Management Automation Network) has been developed by the Los Angeles Police Department to help solve murders.

———————— **SCIENCE AND NATURE** ————————

- The brachiosaurus had a heart the size of a pick-up truck.

- Drinking water after eating reduces the acid in your mouth by 61%.

- The Sumerians of Mesopotamia (c. 3000 BC) thought that the liver made blood and the heart was the centre of thought.

- A rhinoceros has three toes encased in a hoof on each foot.

- Other than humans black lemurs are the only primates that may have blue eyes.

- The average human bladder can hold 13 fluid ounces (approx. 0.4 litres) of liquid.

- Bacteria increase from one to one billion in a Petri dish in 24 hours.

- Rabbits can run at up to 45 mph (72 kph).

- Liquid helium, at a temperature just above absolute zero, can flow upwards.

SCIENCE AND NATURE

- Although there are an estimated ten trillion stars in our galaxy, only some 3,000 of them are visible with the naked eye from earth.

- Glass is a highly viscous liquid.

- The miacis, the ancestor of the dog, had retractable claws and climbed trees when it roamed the earth 40 million years ago.

- Only one satellite has ever been destroyed by a meteor – the European Space Agency's *Olympus* in 1993.

- Scientists in Canada discovered during tests that chickens increase their egg output when pop music is being played.

- Dog food is the most profitable in the supermarket. People spend four times the amount on dog food as they do on baby food.

- Rhinos belong to the same family as horses and are thought to have inspired the myth of the unicorn.

- The largest order of mammals is rodents with about 1,700 species.

————— SCIENCE AND NATURE —————

- Any free-moving liquid will form itself into a sphere in outer space because of its surface tension.

- The black-and-white spots of Holstein dairy cattle are like fingerprints: no two cows have the same pattern of spots.

- The California sea otter grasps its mate's nose in its teeth while copulating.

- Camel milk is the only milk that doesn't curdle when boiled.

- The sperm whale's brain weighs up to 20 lb (9 kg), which is six times heavier than a human's and is the heaviest of all the mammals.

- The billionth decimal digit of the numerical value pi is 9.

- We still retain some of our caveman ancestors' reactions. That is why our hair stands on end when we are frightened: it is a reaction meant to scare off your enemy by making you look taller.

- The little hole in the sink that lets the water drain out instead of flowing over the side is called the porcelator.

SCIENCE AND NATURE

- Following one appeal in Kent for people to hand in all their unused drugs, enough strychnine was handed in on one day in Folkestone to kill the entire population of East Kent.

- Jumping spiders have been found at a height of 22,000 ft (6,705 m) on Mount Everest.

- In the United States 12,500 puppies are born every hour.

- The arteries and veins surrounding the brainstem look like a stick person with the blood vessels called the Circle of Willis forming a large head.

- The majority of spiders belong to the 'orb weaver' spider family Aranidae – pronounced 'a rainy day'.

- To keep cool, ostriches urinate on their legs. The urine then evaporates like sweat.

- A starfish doesn't have a brain.

- A lion's roar can be heard from five miles away.

- Boanthropy is a type of insanity in which a man thinks he is an ox.

————————— **SCIENCE AND NATURE** —————————

- You can tell the age of a fish by the number of growth rings on each of its scales.

- The female ferret is called a jill.

- Winters were colder a thousand years ago. In 1063 the River Thames froze for fourteen weeks.

- An iguana can hold its breath for 28 minutes.

- The so-called 'wild' horses of North America are actually feral animals – free-living descendants of domestic horses that escaped or were turned loose.

- The largest-known kidney stone weighed 1.36 kg.

- The most sensitive finger is the forefinger.

- Sixty per cent of babies are born before breakfast.

- After a flash of lightning the sound of the thunder travels to you at about a mile every five seconds. This allows you to calculate how distant the storm is.

- It would be possible to boil 30 litres of water with the heat generated by the average adult human each day.

SCIENCE AND NATURE

- An instrument developed at the University of Arizona by Dr Frank Low for taking temperature readings of distant planets was so sensitive it was capable of detecting a lit cigarette 10,000 miles (16,093 km) away.

- Dogs are mentioned fourteen times in the Bible.

- You are more likely to get stung by a bee in windy weather than in any other weather condition.

- Murphy's Oil Soap is the chemical most commonly used to clean elephants.

- The tongue is the only muscle in your body that is attached at only one end.

- From one giant redwood, or sequoia, it would be possible to build 60 average-sized houses. The trees can grow to over 300 ft (91 m) in height and 25 ft (7 m) in diameter.

- Cats have five pads on their front feet and only four on their back feet.

- Humans are the only primates that do not have pigment in the palms of their hands.

————————— **SCIENCE AND NATURE** —————————

- The oldest-known goldfish lived to 41 years of age. Its name was Fred.

- The only breed of dog that has a black, rather than a pink, tongue is a chow.

- Surgeons perform better during operations if they are listening to music.

- When a chimpanzee's daubed prints were submitted in a test folio in Pretoria in place of a student's work, they were given a pass mark by the examiners.

- In a survey of 80,000 American women it was found that those who drank moderately had only half the heart-attack risk of those who didn't drink at all.

- The muscle with the longest name in the human body is the *levator labii superioris alaeque nasi* – one of the muscles of facial expression acting on the mouth and nose.

- A humpback whale's milk is 54% fat.

- The strength of early lasers was measured in Gillettes – the number of razor blades a given beam could puncture.

--- **SCIENCE AND NATURE** ---

● Honeybees maintain a temperature of 94°F (34°C) in their hives all year round.

● Nose prints are the most reliable way of identifying dogs.

● The longest recorded flight of a chicken was thirteen seconds.

● Compact discs read from the inside to the outside edge – the reverse of how a record works.

● Iguanas, koalas and Komodo dragons all have two penises.

● A cat has 32 muscles in each ear.

● There are enough explosives on earth to annihilate mankind 50,000 times over.

● Spider monkeys like banana daiquiris.

● A human mucus membrane, which is used to smell, is the size of a first-class postage stamp.

● Identical twins do not have identical fingerprints.

● The human tooth has about 55 miles (89 km) of canals in it.

SCIENCE AND NATURE

- The cracks in breaking glass move at seven times the speed of sound.

- Emus and kangaroos cannot walk backwards, and for that reason they are featured on the Australian coat of arms.

- Bees must visit some 5,000 flowers to make a single spoonful of honey.

- According to a Gallup poll, 29% of people find the Christmas holidays more stressful than enjoyable.

- Every year the earth becomes about 12 tons (12,193 kg) heavier because of meteorites landing.

- The only dog mentioned by name in a Shakespeare play is Crab in *Two Gentlemen of Verona*.

- When you sneeze all your bodily functions stop – including the heart.

- Nearly one in four people finds they have more headaches during the Christmas season than at any other time of year.

- The world pig population is approximately 857,100,000.

SCIENCE AND NATURE

- A pig's orgasm lasts for 30 minutes.

- The smallest fish in the world is the *Trimattum Nanus* of the *Chagos Archipelago*. It measures just 0.33 inches (0.8 cm) long.

- Cat's urine glows in black light.

- A 150-lb (68-kg) adult on earth would weigh 250 tons (254,013 kg) on the sun.

- A human hair is 10,000 times thicker than the film of a soap bubble.

- Apples, not caffeine, are more efficient at waking you up in the morning.

- The blood of an octopus is pale blueish green.

- It takes only 7 lb (3 kg) of pressure to rip off your ear.

- The human heart creates enough pressure to squirt blood 30 ft (9 m).

- The muzzle of a lion is like a fingerprint: no two lions have the same pattern of whiskers.

SCIENCE AND NATURE

- Without an atmosphere the surface temperature on earth at the equator would be 80°C by day and fall to −140°C at night.

- A gruntle is the best word to describe the snout of a pig.

- Dogs like squeezy toys because they sound like animals in distress.

- The spots of light you see when you rub your eyes are called phosphenes.

- So far man has survived on earth for two million years. The dinosaurs lasted 150 million years.

- The average computer user blinks seven times a minute.

- The first fish in space was a South American guppy in 1976.

- Ferrets can sleep for up to twenty hours a day.

- Extremely loud sounds, when properly directed, can actually bore holes through solid matter.

- A rat can survive longer without water than a camel.

SCIENCE AND NATURE

- After human death, post-mortem rigidity starts in the head, travels to the feet and leaves the same way it came – head to toe.

- A type of jellyfish found off the coast of England is the longest animal in the world.

- A cat's jaws cannot move sideways.

- The average cost of a white laboratory mouse is 65p.

- Bowerbirds of Australia and New Guinea decorate their courting grounds with everything from beetle wings to car keys.

- The wolverine is the largest member of the weasel family.

- A UN survey revealed that postmen in Britain are bitten by dogs far less than in any other country.

- It took a 19th-century Danish schoolmaster a lifetime to calculate pi to 800 decimal places. It took a modern computer only a few seconds to check his figures and find them correct.

- Basenji dogs and Australian dingoes are virtually identical.

——————— SCIENCE AND NATURE ———————

- A hedgehog's heart beats 300 times a minute on average.

- A tiger's paw prints are called pug marks.

- Giraffes have no vocal cords.

- Emus have double-plumed feathers and they lay emerald/forest green eggs.

- The permanent teeth that erupt to replace the baby teeth are called succedaneous teeth.

- A great horned owl can turn its head 270°.

- The white area at the base of a fingernail is called the lunula.

- In the last 3,000 years no new animals have been domesticated.

- The pet ferret was domesticated more than 500 years before the house cat.

- In England it was once considered sacrilege to kill a bee, which was regarded as the holiest of insects.

--------------------- **SCIENCE AND NATURE** ---------------------

● A pig's skin is thickest on its back, where it can be up to ⅙ inch (0.4 cm) thick.

● Calling a puppy to punish it teaches it not to come when it's called. It is best to reward a dog by bringing it to you – and to punish it by sending it away.

● Montana mountain goats butt heads so hard their hooves fall off.

● More than 30 million people in the US suffer from diastema – a gap between the two upper front teeth.

● Societies in ancient Rome, Germany and China used urine as a mouthwash.

● Crows have the largest cerebral hemispheres relative to their body size of any avian family.

● Babies dream in the womb, according to medical experts.

● Two out of every five women in the US dye their hair.

● When you cross cattle with buffalo you get a beefalo.

● An average housefly lives for one month.

SCIENCE AND NATURE

- Dalmatian dogs are born pure white. Their spots don't appear until they are three or four days old.

- Armadillos and humans are the only animals that can get leprosy.

- If you feed a seagull Alka Seltzer its stomach will explode.

- An estimated 80% of animals on earth have six legs.

- Skin temperature does not go much above 95°F (35°C) even on the hottest day.

- Mosquitoes are attracted to the colour blue more than twice as much as to any other single colour.

- If the eggs spawned by all the female cod in one season survived they would fill the oceans from seabed to surface. Cod lay between four and five million eggs at a time – but usually only about five survive.

- Flying fish 'fly' at between 35 and 45 mph (56 and 72 kph).

- Thumbnails grow much more slowly than fingernails.

- One human hair can support 3 kg.

SCIENCE AND NATURE

- A teaspoonful of neutron star material would weigh about 110 million tons (111,760,000 tonnes).

- One Australian wasp has the scientific name *Aha ha*.

- Seven per cent of the entire Irish barley crop goes to the production of Guinness.

- Your hearing becomes less sharp after eating too much.

- Slugs travel at a top speed of .007 mph (.011 kph), can stretch to eleven times their length and have 27,000 teeth to help eat their food

- When the walkie-talkie was first introduced commercially, in 1934, it was described as a 'portable super-regenerative receiver and transmitter'.

- Sharks can detect the heartbeats of other fish.

- Women suffer more tooth decay than men do.

- The tip of an elephant's trunk is so sensitive and flexible that it can pick up a pin.

- The Winter Banana is actually an apple.

SCIENCE AND NATURE

- In 1902 the British horse population was three and a half million. It required fifteen million acres (6,075,000 hectares) to provide their food and they produced ten million tons (10,160,000 tonnes) of manure a year.

- A female bed bug has survived 565 days without food.

- The first Rolls Royce, marketed in 1906, sold for £400. Now it would fetch £150,000 plus.

- Most elephants weigh less than the tongue of the Blue Whale.

- Doctors in Florida found that patients undergoing certain operations bled twice as quickly when the moon was in its second quarter.

- An elephant can smell water 3 miles (5 km) away.

- Neither horses nor rabbits can vomit.

- The first Ford cars had Dodge engines.

- Water, which boils at 100°C at sea level, will boil at 70°C at the top of Mount Everest.

SCIENCE AND NATURE

- Ingrown toenails are hereditary.

- A male emperor moth can smell a female up to 7 miles (11 km) away.

- A shark can detect one part of blood in 100 million parts of water.

- A cat has four rows of whiskers.

- Armadillos have four babies at a time and they are always all the same sex.

- A pelican can hold about 25 lb (11 kg) of fish in its pouch.

- The only insect that can turn its head is a praying mantis.

- The top speed of the Zamboni ice-resurfacing machine is 14 kph (9 mph).

- In the Caribbean there are oysters that can climb trees.

- There are 613 commandments in the Old Testament and the wild pomegranate is said to contain that exact number of seeds.

SCIENCE AND NATURE

- Cows break wind sixteen times a day and produce around 65 lb (29 kg) of manure.

- No one knows why a duck's quack doesn't echo.

- The common garden worm has five pairs of hearts.

- The dog's mucus membrane is the size of 50 postage stamps.

- Eighty per cent of the world's food crops are pollinated by insects.

- When *Voyager 2* visited Neptune it filmed a small, irregular white triangle that zips around Neptune's surface every sixteen hours or so and is now known as the Scooter.

- Each day 4 ½ lb (2 kg) of sunlight strike the earth.

- There are more beetles than any other creature in the world.

- It is illegal in Alaska to give a moose an alcoholic drink.

- Armadillos can walk under water.

--------- **SCIENCE AND NATURE** ---------

• The common goldfish is the only animal that can see both infrared and ultraviolet light.

• When penguins hop on to an ice floe they always choose one that will take them back to land.

• The growth rate of some bamboo plants can reach 3 ft (0.9 m) a day.

• Dalmatian dogs originate from the Dalmatian coast of Croatia.

• Armadillos can be housebroken.

• The smartest dogs are (in order of intelligence): Border collies, poodles and golden retrievers.

• The lining of your digestive system is shed every three days.

• It is impossible to sneeze with your eyes open.

• The word rodent comes from the Latin word *rodere*, which means 'to gnaw'.

• The human brain stops growing at the age of eighteen.

SCIENCE AND NATURE

- The only way to stop the pain of a flathead fish's sting is by rubbing its slime on the wound it gave you.

- There is now 841.6 lb (381.7 kg) of the moon on the earth. That is the amount of rock and soil brought back by American astronauts on their six expeditions there.

- Toy dog breeds live an average seven years longer than large breeds.

- The longest recorded life span of a camel was 35 years and five months.

- Chewing gum while peeling onions will keep you from crying.

- A grass snake can move at 4.2 mph (6.8 kph).

- Nutmeg is extremely poisonous if injected intravenously.

- An elephant's trunk can hold four gallons of water.

- A group of hares is called a husk.

- A group of goats is called a trip.

SCIENCE AND NATURE

- A group of larks is called an exaltation.

- Solid hydrogen is the densest substance in the world at 70.6 g/cc.

- A bumblebee beats its wings 160 times a second.

- Every hamster in the US today comes from a single litter captured in Syria in 1930.

- The microwave was invented after a researcher walked by a radar tube and a chocolate bar melted in his pocket.

- Your stomach has to produce a new layer of mucus every two weeks or it will digest itself.

- Every part of the hemlock plant is deadly poisonous – the flowers, leaves, roots, stems and seeds.

- Termites eat through wood twice as fast when listening to rock music.

- Orcas kill sharks by torpedoing up into the shark's stomach from underneath, causing the shark to explode.

- A peanut is not a nut, it is a legume.

--- **SCIENCE AND NATURE** ---

- Each year the moon's orbit moves about 1.5 inches (3.8 cm) further away from the earth.

- If you were ejected into space, you would explode before you suffocated because there is no air pressure.

- The two most common surgeries are biopsies and Caesarean sections.

- The 2-ft-long (0.6-m) New Zealand mountain bird kea likes to eat the strips of rubber around car windows.

- Potatoes were banned in Burgundy in 1910 because it was believed frequent eating could cause leprosy.

- Scientists working on the Manhattan Project in the early 1940s measured the time it took for an imploding shell of uranium to reach critical mass and initiate spontaneous fission in 'shakes of a lamb's tail'. One 'shake' equalled 1×10^{-8} s (one hundred millionth of a second). It took about three shakes of a lamb's tail.

- You can tell a turtle's gender by the noise it makes: males grunt, females hiss.

- Owls are the only birds that can see the colour blue.

SCIENCE AND NATURE

- The Airedale dog was originally known as a waterside terrier.

- Cats in Halifax, Nova Scotia, Canada, have a very high probability of having six toes.

- The little lump of flesh just forward of the ear canal and immediately next to the temple is called a tragus.

- Lady Coventry was an early victim of cosmetics. She died in October 1760 from the poisonous effects of regularly painting her face with white lead.

- Women's hearts beat faster than do men's.

- The 1-oz brown bat, which is most common in North America, is capable of eating 500 insects an hour during its night-time feeding.

- St Bernard dogs do not carry kegs of brandy and never have.

- You burn more calories sleeping than watching television.

- Some carnivores, rodents, bats and insectivores have a penis bone called a baculum.

—————— SCIENCE AND NATURE ——————

- Jellyfish are the wettest creatures on earth, being made up of 95.4% water. An average adult human has a water content of just over 60%.

- The only bone not connected to another bone in the human body is in the throat, at the back of the tongue.

- The oldest tortoise lived to the age of 152.

- Since 1600 a total of 109 species and subspecies of bird have become extinct.

- Jackals have one more pair of chromosomes than dogs or wolves.

- You can tell the sex of a crab by its stomach: the female's is beehive-shaped, while the male's is lighthouse-shaped.

- A full-grown bear can run as fast as a horse over short distances.

- The name of fungal remains found in coal is sclerotinite.

- The largest-known mountain in the solar system is on Mars and is called Olympus Mons. It is a volcano three times the height of Everest.

SCIENCE AND NATURE

- The sparrow was imported to New York in 1850 to cope with an excess of tree worms.

- The anteater, aardvark, spiny anteater and scaly anteater are completely unrelated. In fact the closest relatives to anteaters are sloths and armadillos. The closest relative to the spiny anteater is the platypus and the aardvark is in an order all by itself.

- The 2.5-ton (2,540-kg), 55-ft-long (17-m) giant squid has the largest eyes of any animal on earth, each being more than a foot (0.3 m) in diameter.

- The smallest unit of time is a yoctosecond.

- One way to tell seals and sea lions apart is that sea lions have external ears and testicles.

- Reindeer like to eat bananas.

- For every extra kilogram carried on a space flight, 530 kg of extra fuel are need at lift-off.

- A normal dog has 42 teeth: 20 in the upper jaw and 22 in the lower jaw. A human adult has 32 teeth equally divided between the two jaws.

--- **SCIENCE AND NATURE** ---

- A fully mature oak tree sheds about 700,000 leaves every year.

- The average person flexes the joints in their fingers 24 million times in their lifetime.

- As of 2002 in New York City rats outnumbered humans by twelve to one.

- The only time in history when the roman numerals in a year were written using all the numerals in order from highest value to lowest value was 1666 – MDCLXVI (1,000 plus 500 plus 100 plus 50 plus 10 plus 5 plus 1).

- There are 62,000 miles (99,777 km) of arteries, veins and blood capillaries in the human body.

- In Hong Kong a red-and-white-striped pole outside a premises may not necessarily indicate a barber's shop. It is also the sign for a brothel.

- A cubic mile of sea water contains, on average, more than £60 million worth of gold and £6 million worth of silver.

- The skin that peels off after sunburn is called blype.

SCIENCE AND NATURE

- In a dental experiment on elephants, motor-car tyres were chopped up and baked in their bread. The elephants never noticed.

- You can avoid sinking in quicksand by lying on your back and raising your legs slowly.

- To be classified as sterling an object must contain 92.5% silver.

- The word 'pixel' is a contraction of 'picture cell' or 'picture element'.

- The northern fur seal has more mates each year than any other mammal. The average male will mate with between 40 and 60 females each season.

- Hot water is heavier than cold water.

- In 1976 the swine flu vaccine caused more deaths than the illness it was intended to prevent.

- A chicken is the only animal that can be eaten before it is born and after it is dead.

- The surface area of an average-sized brick is 79 sq. cm.

SCIENCE AND NATURE

- If you were locked in a completely sealed room you would die of carbon dioxide poisoning before oxygen deprivation.

- Ants cannot chew their food; they move their jaws sideways like scissors to extract juices from it.

- You can tell the age of a mountain goat by the number of rings on its small, black horns.

- The Jack Russell terrier was named after English church minister the Reverend John Russell.

- Peanuts are one of the ingredients of dynamite.

- Your thumb is the same length as your nose.

- Eighty per cent of the average human brain is water.

- In the US, 40 people every minute are sent to hospital for dog bites.

- A woman who returned a book to the Stroud Library, in Gloucestershire, England, in a very tattered state explained it was the fault of her dog, which had chewed it. The name of the book was *How to Train Your Dog*.

SCIENCE AND NATURE

- Honeybees have hair on their eyes.

- Very tall buildings naturally lean towards the course of the sun.

- Most spiders have eight eyes.

- Cats have more than 100 vocal sounds, while dogs only have about ten.

- Spiders do not get caught in their own webs because they cover themselves with a greasy anti-silk film.

- Some female hyenas have a pseudo penis.

- Depending on the type of grasshopper, its 'ears' are located either on its forelegs or on the base of its abdomen.

- Twelve or more cows are known as a flink.

- One inch (2.5 cm) of rain has the same water equivalent as 10 inches (25 cm) of snow.

- The ragdoll is the largest breed of domesticated cat in the world, with adult males averaging from 22 to 25 lb (10–11 kg).

SCIENCE AND NATURE

- An ostrich's eye is bigger than its brain.

- A South American termite queen can produce 30,000 eggs in a day and do this daily for up to a year. A colony of more than five million termites can come from a single queen.

- The longest recorded lifespan of a slug is eighteen months.

- An adult electric eel can produce up to 600 volts – sufficient to stun a grown horse.

- The world's elephants could drink dry the Serpentine lake in Hyde Park, London, if they all supped at the same time.

- When press tycoon William Randolph Hearst sent a telegram to a leading astronomer asking if there was life on Mars and to please cable 1,000 words on the subject, he received the reply: 'Nobody knows' repeated 500 times.

- The antibiotic nystatin, which is used chiefly to treat fungal infections such as thrush, is named after New York State, where it was developed.

- The average housefly lives for one month.

─────── SCIENCE AND NATURE ───────

- A whale's penis is called a dork.

- Dibble means to drink like a duck.

- The difference between fowl and poultry is that poultry are domesticated fowl.

- In Australia the male antechinus mouse has up to sixteen partners a time in sex sessions in trees lasting up to twelve hours. Often they become so weak they fall out of the trees and are killed.

- The longest known record for constipation is 102 days.

- The storage capacity of a human brain exceeds 4 terrabytes.

- It takes seven years for a lobster to grow to 1 lb (0.4 kg).

- There are 45 miles (72 km) of nerves in the human body.

- A sow will always have an even number of teats or nipples – usually twelve.

- The heaviest organs in the human body are the lungs, which together weigh about 42 oz (approx. 1,176 g).

SCIENCE AND NATURE

- Hamsters love to eat crickets.

- The holes are put in fly swatters to lower air resistance.

- A cross between a greyhound and a terrier is a whippet.

- Lycanthropy is a disease in which a man thinks he's a wolf. It is the scientific name for wolfman or werewolf.

- You lose enough dead skin cells in your lifetime to fill eight 5-lb (2 kg) flour bags.

- Babies are born without kneecaps. They do not appear until the child reaches two to six years of age.

- Insects in India each year eat more food than the entire human population of London.

- Dentists recommend that a toothbrush be kept at least 6 ft (1.8 m) away from a toilet to avoid airborne particles resulting from the flush.

- The female praying mantis is such a deadly hunter that she often eats her partner immediately after mating. Sometimes she begins her meal while they are still copulating.

SCIENCE AND NATURE

- The world's termites outweigh the world's humans by 10 to 1.

- Shrews and platypuses are the only mammals that are poisonous.

- The word 'lethologica' means an inability to recall words – commonly indicated by the expression 'It's on the tip of my tongue ...'

- Butterflies taste with their feet.

- The world's smallest mammal is the bumblebee bat of Thailand, weighing less than a penny.

- Roosters cannot crow if they are not able to fully extend their necks.

- The strongest surface winds in the solar system are found on Neptune, where they have been measured at 1,500 mph (2,414 kph).

- A third of all cancers are sun-related.

- A sneeze travels out of your mouth at over 100 mph (161 kph).

SCIENCE AND NATURE

- Balding men going to hair clinics have an average age of 24 years and 5 months.

- An average adult human being has around 2,381,248 sweat glands on their skin.

- The average talker sprays about 300 microscopic saliva drops per minute – about 2.5 droplets per word.

- On take-off an *Apollo* spacecraft develops more power than all the cars in Britain put together.

- The parachute was invented by Leonardo da Vinci in 1515.

- So important to human dexterity is the thumb that the brain devotes a larger portion to controlling it than to controlling the chest and abdomen.

- In 1908 the leaning tower of Pisa officially weighed 14,486 tons (14,718 tonnes). By 1973 it was officially slimmed to 14,200 tons (14,427 tonnes).

- The straw was developed by Egyptian brewers to taste beer without removing the fermenting ingredients that floated on the top of the container.

———— SCIENCE AND NATURE ————

- When female elephants have been pregnant for more than twenty months and are still not in labour they will travel a hundred miles searching for the leaves of the boraginaceae tree – which can also induce birth in humans.

- There are 450 hairs in an average eyebrow.

- A quarter of all mammal species are bats.

- Studies show that if a cat falls off the seventh floor of a building it has about a 30% less chance of surviving than a cat that falls off the twentieth floor. It takes about eight floors for the cat to realise what is happening, relax and correct itself.

- In a single night a mole can tunnel 220 ft (67 m).

- In 1977 a thirteen–year–old child found a tooth growing out of his left foot.

- Gentlemen in the eighteenth century used cork pads, or plumpers, to fill out the hollows left in their cheeks by the loss of rotten teeth.

- A shrimp's heart is in its head.

-------------- SCIENCE AND NATURE --------------

- Every night the parrot fish sleeps inside a mucus cocoon, which it constructs daily to block its body smell from predators.

- Most hamsters blink one eye at a time.

- The opening to the cave in which a bear hibernates is always on a northern slope.

- Your right lung takes in more air than your left lung.

- A shark is the only fish that can blink with both eyes.

- Two centuries ago a newborn baby had less chance of surviving a week than a person of 90.

- There are more than 100 million light-sensitive cells in each of your retinas.

- Human birth-control pills work on gorillas.

- The cells that make up the antlers of a moose are the fastest-growing animal cells in nature.

- The average person inhales at about force 2 (a light breeze) on the wind-strength Beaufort scale.

——————— **SCIENCE AND NATURE** ———————

- The underside of a horse's hoof is called a frog. The frog peels off several times a year to be replaced by a new growth.

- A dragonfly has a lifespan of just 24 hours.

- Baby robins eat 14 ft (4 m) of earthworms a day.

- Pearls melt in vinegar.

- Mill Reef, the famous racehorse, received more than 30 get-well cards a day after fracturing a foreleg.

- In his book *The Insects* naturalist Url N Lanham reports that the aphid reproduction cycle is so rapid that the females are born pregnant.

- In 1872 locals in North Yorkshire recorded that a swarm of ladybirds took three days to pass.

- Hippopotamuses make 80% of their vocalisations under water.

- Even with its favourite food laid out to tempt it, a giant tortoise can manage a top speed of only five yards (4.5 m) a minute – 0.17 mph (0.2 kph).

SCIENCE AND NATURE

- The honey badger can withstand hundreds of African bee stings that would kill any other animal.

- It would take seven billion particles of fog to fill a teaspoon.

- You blink over ten million times a year.

- A rat can chew through just about any building material, including concrete.

- Men get hiccups more often than women do.

- Alligators cannot move backwards.

- Some ribbon worms will eat themselves if they cannot find food.

- A pig always sleeps on its right side.

- When opossums are playing 'possum' they are not playing but have passed out from sheer terror.

- If you divide the Great Pyramid's perimeter by twice its height you get pi to the fifteenth digit.

- Women blink twice as often as men do.

---------------- **SCIENCE AND NATURE** ----------------

- The rattlesnake has the best heat–detecting equipment in nature. Using the two organs between its eyes and nostrils it can locate a mouse by its body heat at a distance of 15 m.

- The archerfish brings down its insect prey with well-aimed mouthfuls of spit. It is even able to compensate for refraction when it shoots from under water.

- EEG stands for electroencephalogram or electroencephalograph.

- Fingernails grow nearly four times faster than toenails.

- The whole of a human's skin weighs twice as much as their brain.

- The world's first dog show took place in Newcastle upon-Tyne in 1859 and attracted an entry of 60 pointers and setters.

- Moths hear through the hairs on their bodies.

- Over a thousand birds a year die from smashing into windows.

- A robin's egg is blue, but if you put it in vinegar for 30 days it turns yellow.

USELESS
THINGS PEOPLE
SAY

——— USELESS THINGS PEOPLE SAY ———

- 'I'm one of those stupid bums who never went to university, and it hasn't done me any harm.'

  Prince Philip

- 'I'm one of those stupid bums who went to university. Well, I think it's helped me.'

  Prince Charles

- 'Children today are tyrants. They contradict their parents, gobble their food and tyrannise their teachers. I despair for the future.'

  Socrates, 400 BC

- 'Outside consultants sought for test of gas chamber.'

  Arizona Republic ad

- 'Those who survived the San Francisco earthquake said: "Thank God I'm still alive." But, of course, those who died, their lives will never be the same again.'

  US Senator Barbara Boxer

- 'Most lies about blondes are false.'

  Cincinnati Times-Star

- 'Maybe this world is another planet's Hell.'

  Aldous Huxley

—— **USELESS THINGS PEOPLE SAY** ——

- 'Cod are not very good swimmers so are easily overtaken by trawlers and nets.'

  Ministry explanation of diminishing North Sea cod

- 'A lie gets halfway around the world before the truth has a chance to get its pants on.'

  Sir Winston Churchill

- 'Most cars on our roads have only one occupant, usually the driver.'

  Carol Malia, BBC TV presenter

- 'The Holocaust was an obscene period in our nation's history. I mean in this century's history. But we all lived in this century. I didn't live in this century.'

  US Vice-President Dan Quayle

- 'I've just learned about his illness. Let's hope it's nothing trivial.'

  US reporter/writer Irvin S Cobb

- Movie star Tallulah Bankhead once described herself as 'Pure as the driven slush'.

- 'The only way to get rid of a temptation is to yield to it.'

  Oscar Wilde

——— USELESS THINGS PEOPLE SAY ———

● 'We are not ready for an unforeseen event that may or may not occur.'

US Vice-President Dan Quayle

● 'In America, anybody can be president. That's one of the risks you take.'

US politican and diplomat Adlai Stevenson

● 'We don't like their sound. Groups of guitars are on the way out.'

Decca Records, speaking about the Beatles

● 'A billion here, a billion there, sooner or later it adds up to real money.'

Congressman Everett Dirksen

● 'You can get more with a kind word and a gun than you can with a kind word alone.'

Al Capone

● 'A man in love is incomplete until he is married. Then he is finished.'

Zsa Zsa Gabor

● 'I worship the quicksand he walks in.'

US political humourist Art Buchwald

———— USELESS THINGS PEOPLE SAY ————

- 'If it weren't for electricity we'd all be watching television by candlelight.'

  US actor/comedian George Gobel

- 'A pessimist sees the difficulty in every opportunity; an optimist sees the opportunity in every difficulty.'

  Sir Winston Churchill

- 'Does the album have any songs you like that aren't on it?'

  Music reviewer Harry News

- 'Fiction writing is great. You can make up almost anything.'

  Ivana Trump – after her first novel was published

- 'We're going to move left and right at the same time.'

  California governor Jerry Brown

- 'The word genius isn't applicable in football. A genius is a guy like Norman Einstein.'

  Sports analyst Joe Theisman

- 'We talked five times. He called me twice and I called him twice.'

  California Angels coach

——— USELESS THINGS PEOPLE SAY ———

- 'If I had as many love affairs as you have given me credit for, I would now be speaking to you from a jar in the Harvard Medical School.'

  Frank Sinatra, speaking to reporters

- 'If you take out the killings, Washington actually has a very low crime rate.'

  The Mayor of Washington

- 'That's just the tip of the ice cube.'

  Former Tory MP Neil Hamilton, speaking on BBC2

- 'Whether you think that you can, or that you can't, you are usually right.'

  Henry Ford

- 'I'd rather be dead than singing "Satisfaction" when I'm 45.'

  Mick Jagger

- 'We are not without accomplishment. We have managed to distribute poverty equally.'

  Vietnam's Foreign Minister

- 'Good-looking people turn me off, myself included.'

  Patrick Swayze

USELESS THINGS PEOPLE SAY

- 'Danger. Slow men at work.'

  Brunei road sign

- 'Never interrupt your enemy when he is making a mistake.'

  Napoleon Bonaparte

- 'Ladies are requested not to have children at the bar.'

  Norwegian bar notice

- 'I may be dumb but I'm not stupid.'

  US Football announcer Terry Bradshaw

- 'The longer I live the more I see that I am never wrong about anything, and that all the pains that I have so humbly taken to verify my notions have only wasted my time.'

  George Bernard Shaw

- 'And as Mansell comes into the pits, he's quite literally sweating his eyeballs out.'

  British TV commentator

- 'My Lord, we find the man who stole the mare not guilty.'

  Welsh jury foreman

—— USELESS THINGS PEOPLE SAY ——

- 'To love oneself is the beginning of a lifelong romance.'

  Oscar Wilde

- 'I patterned my look after Cinderella, Mother Goose and the local hooker.'

  Dolly Parton, speaking in an interview

- The *two types of men* Mae West said she preferred 'Domestic and foreign.'

- 'It was not my kind of people. There wasn't a producer, a press agent, a director or an actor.'

  Zsa Zsa Gabor, about her trial jury

- 'Hi, I'm Dean White. Dick of the college.'

  Duke University dean Richard White

- 'I invented the internet.'

  US Vice-President Al Gore

- 'Most hotels are already booked solid by people, plus 5,000 journalists.'

  Bangkok Post

- *'Life is very important to Americans.'*

  US Senator Bob Dole

——— USELESS THINGS PEOPLE SAY ———

- 'My favourite programme is *Mrs Dale's Diary*. I try never to miss it because it is the only way of knowing what goes on in a middle-class family.'

  The Queen Mother

- 'If you walk backwards, you'll find out that you can go forwards and people won't know if you're coming or going.'

  Baseball manager Casey Stengel

- 'The team has come along slow but fast.'

  Baseball manager Casey Stengel

- 'People that are really very weird can get into sensitive positions and have a tremendous impact on history.'

  US Vice-President Dan Quayle

- 'And now the sequence of events in no particular order.'

  CBS news anchorman Dan Rather

- 'Weather forecast: Precipitation in the morning, rain in the afternoon.'

  Detroit Daily News

- 'Make everything as simple as possible, but not simpler.'

  Albert Einstein

—— USELESS THINGS PEOPLE SAY ——

- 'You'd better learn secretarial work – or else get married.'
  Model agent Emmeline Strively, speaking to
  Marilyn Monroe in 1944

- 'I've read about foreign policy and studied – I know the number of continents.'
  US presidential candidate George Wallace

- 'It is white.'
  President George W Bush, describing the White House

- 'The true measure of a man is how he treats someone who can do him absolutely no good.'
  Samuel Johnson

- 'Teeth extracted by the latest Methodists.'
  Hong Kong dental ad

- 'I don't like this word "bomb". It is not a bomb but a device that is exploding.'
  French Ambassador Jacques Leblanc,
  speaking on nuclear weapons

- 'I find that the harder I work, the more luck I seem to have.'
  US President Thomas Jefferson

───── USELESS THINGS PEOPLE SAY ─────

● 'When choosing between two evils, I always like to try the one I've never tried before.'

Mae West

● 'In a sense it's a one-man show. Except there are two men involved.'

John Motson, BBC sports commentator

● 'Only two things are infinite, the universe and human stupidity, and I'm not sure about the former.'

Albert Einstein

● 'I don't diet. I just don't eat as much as I'd like to.'

Supermodel Linda Evangelista

● 'I used to be Snow White, but I drifted.'

Mae West

● 'Now there's a broad with her future behind her.'

Fellow performer Constance Bennett, describing the young Marilyn Monroe

● 'Politics gives guys so much power that they tend to behave badly around women. And I hope I never get into that.'

US President Bill Clinton

──── USELESS THINGS PEOPLE SAY ────

- 'I don't know anything about music. In my line you don't have to.'

  Elvis Presley

- 'Pitching is 80% of the game. The other half is hitting and fielding.'

  Baseball player Mickey Rivers

- 'I think you can't repeat the first time of something.'

  Singer Natalie Imbruglia

- 'Glory is fleeting, but obscurity is forever.'

  Napoleon Bonaparte

- 'Sometimes they write what I say and not what I mean.'

  Baseball player Pedro Guerrero – about the press

- When John Houston cast his daughter, Anjelica, in a leading role in *A Walk with Love and Death* – her film debut – she was panned by the critics. One wrote: 'She has the face of an exhausted gnu, the voice of an unstrung tennis racket and a figure of no describable shape.'

- 'Permitted vehicles not allowed.'

  Road sign on US Highway 27

——— USELESS THINGS PEOPLE SAY ———

● 'Wonderful bargains for men with 16 and 17 necks.'

Clothing store sign

● 'If history repeats itself I should think we can expect the same thing again.'

Terry Venables

● 'We didn't lose. We weren't beaten. We just came in second.'

US commentator at 1996 Olympics

● 'I've never had major knee surgery on any other part of my body.'

Basketball player Winston Bennet

● 'To make women learned and foxes tame has the same defect – to make them more cunning.'

King James I

● 'How would you like to make a thousand speeches and never once be allowed to say what you think yourself?'

King Edward VIII to Churchill

● 'If you can count your money, you don't have a billion dollars.'

J Paul Getty

——— USELESS THINGS PEOPLE SAY ———

- 'I really didn't say everything I said.'
  'Always go to other people's funerals, otherwise they won't go to yours.'
  'It's like déjà vu all over again.'
  'Predictions are difficult, especially about the future.'
  'A nickel ain't worth a dime any more.'

  Baseball player Yogi Berra

- 'You look after your Empire and I will look after my life.'

  Princess Margaret – after being reproached by the Queen

- 'Whenever I watch TV and I see those poor starving kids all over the world, I can't help but cry. I mean I would love to be skinny like that, but not with all those flies and death and stuff.'

  Singer Mariah Carey

- 'If women didn't exist, all the money in the world would have no meaning.'

  Aristotle Onassis

- 'The doctors X-rayed my head and found nothing.'

  Baseball player Dizzy Dean

- 'The covers of this book are too far apart.'

  US newspaper columnist and novelist Ambrose Bierce

USELESS THINGS PEOPLE SAY

- 'I shall go back to bed. I have never slept with a Queen before.'

    King William IV — on acceding to the throne

- 'Knowledge speaks, but wisdom listens.'

    Jimi Hendrix

- 'Sure there have been injuries and deaths in boxing, but none of them serious.'

    Boxer Alan Minter

- 'Whatever is begun in anger ends in shame.'

    US statesman and scientist Benjamin Franklin

- 'I wish men had boobs because I like the feel of them. It's so funny, when I record I sing with a hand over each of them. Maybe it's a comfort thing.'

    Singer Emma Bunton (Baby Spice)

- 'The internet is a great way to get on the net.'

    US presidential candidate Bob Dole

- 'Hawaii is a unique state. It is a state that is by itself. It is different from the other 49 states. Well, all states are different, but it's got a particularly unique situation.'

    US Vice-President Dan Quayle

──── USELESS THINGS PEOPLE SAY ────

- 'I am often asked whether it is through some genetic trait that I stand with my hands behind my back like my father. The answer is that we both have the same tailor. He makes our sleeves so tight that we can't get our hands in front.'

  Prince Charles

- 'You got to be careful if you don't know where you're going, because you might not get there.'

  Baseball player Yogi Berra

- 'My sister's expecting a baby, and I don't know if I'm going to be an uncle or an aunt.'

  Basketball player Chuck Nevitt

- 'Reality is merely an illusion, albeit a very persistent one.'

  Albert Einstein

- 'If you give a person a fish, they'll fish for a day. But if you train a person to fish, they'll fish for a lifetime.'

  US Vice-President Dan Quayle

- 'Our strength is we don't have any weaknesses. Our weakness is that we don't have any real strengths.'

  College football coach Frank Broyles

———— USELESS THINGS PEOPLE SAY ————

- 'We don't necessarily discriminate. We simply exclude certain types of people.'

  US colonel Gerald Wellman

- 'Many a man's reputation would not know his character if they met on the street.'

  US author Elbert Hubbard

- 'The people in the navy look on motherhood as being compatible with being a woman.'

  Rear Admiral James R Hogg

- 'I have no political ambitions for myself or my children.'

  Former US Ambassador to Great Britain
  Joseph P Kennedy, 1936

- 'He's a guy who gets up at six o'clock in the morning regardless of what time it is.'

  Boxing trainer Lou Duva

- 'God's wounds! I will pull down my breeches and they shall also see my arse.'

  King James I – when told the public wished to see him

- 'Who the hell wants to hear actors talk?'

  Warner Brothers, 1927

────── USELESS THINGS PEOPLE SAY ──────

- 'It's like when I buy a horse. I don't want a thick neck and short legs.'

  Mickey Rourke – on his ideal woman

- 'If people get a kick out of running down pedestrians, you have to let them do it.'

  Video-game director Paul Jacobs

- 'He dribbles a lot and the opposition don't like it. You can see it all over their faces.'
  'I would not say David Ginola is the best left-winger in the Premiership, but there are none better.'

  Ron Atkinson

- 'I have been trained in private never to show emotion in public.'

  The Queen

- 'Solutions are not the answer.'

  US President Richard Nixon

- 'Happiness is good health and a bad memory.'

  Ingrid Bergman

- 'We live above the shop.'

  Prince Philip

———— USELESS THINGS PEOPLE SAY ————

- 'I favour access to discrimination on the basis of sexual orientation.'

  US Senator Ted Kennedy

- 'He treats us like men. He lets us wear earrings.'

  Houston sportsman Tonin Polk

- 'The object of war is not to die for your country but to make the other bastard die for his.'

  General George Patton

- 'The art world thinks of me as an uncultured, polo-playing clot.'

  Prince Philip

- 'During the scrimmage Tarkanian paced the sideline with his hands in his pockets while biting his nails.'

  Associated Press report

- 'I'm all in favour of keeping dangerous weapons out of the hands of fools. Let's start with typewriters.'

  US architect Frank Lloyd Wright

- 'We princes are set, as it were, upon stages in the sight and view of all the world.'

  Queen Elizabeth I

——— USELESS THINGS PEOPLE SAY ———

● 'Next up is the Central African Republic, located in Central Africa.'

> *Australian sports commentator Bob Costas*

● 'China is a big country, inhabited by many Chinese.'

> *French President Charles de Gaulle*

● 'Morcelli has four fastest 1,500-metre times ever. And all those times are at 1,500 metres.'

> *Sports commentator David Coleman*

● 'I deny the allegations and I deny the alligators.'

> *Chicago alderman when indicted*

● 'Be nice to people on your way up because you meet them on your way down.'

> *US actor and piano player Jimmy Durante*

● 'Sit by the homely girl, you'll look better by comparison.'

> *Miss America 1983 – Debra Maffett*

● 'God gave men both a penis and a brain, but unfortunately not enough blood supply to run both at the same time.'

> *Robin Williams, commenting on the Clinton sex scandal*

——— USELESS THINGS PEOPLE SAY ———

- 'If everything seems under control, you're just not going fast enough.'

  Grand Prix legend Mario Andretti

- 'Strangely, in slow-motion replay, the ball seemed to hang in the air for even longer.'

  Sports commentator David Acfield

- 'I think "Hail to the Chief" has a nice ring to it.'

  John F Kennedy – when asked to name his favourite song

- 'We're just physically not physical enough.'

  Basketball coach Denny Crum

- 'I have as much privacy as a goldfish in a bowl.'

  Princess Margaret

- 'I don't want to achieve immortality through my work; I want to achieve immortality through not dying.'

  Woody Allen

- 'A period novel about the civil war? Who needs the civil war now? Who cares?'

  Pictorial Review editor when offered Gone with the Wind serialisation in 1936

——— USELESS THINGS PEOPLE SAY ———

- 'Boxing is all about getting the job done as quickly as possible, whether it takes 10 or 15 or 20 rounds.'

  Frank Bruno

- 'Models are like baseball players. We make a lot of money quickly, but all of a sudden we're 30 years old, we don't have a college education, we're qualified for nothing, and we're used to a very nice lifestyle. The best thing is to marry a movie star.'

  Supermodel Cindy Crawford

- 'I'm living so far beyond my income that we may almost be said to be living apart.'

  US poet E E Cummings

- 'If you think it was an accident, applaud.'

  US journalist and talk-show host Geraldo Rivera, speaking to his TV audience on Natalie Wood's drowning

- 'If I were two-faced, would I be wearing this one?'

  Abraham Lincoln

- 'If you haven't got anything nice to say about anybody, come sit next to me.'

  Alice Roosevelt Longworth

—— USELESS THINGS PEOPLE SAY ——

● 'The Queen's [Victoria's] bosom has been deliciously handled and has been brought out by the artist in full rotundity.'

The Times art critic

● 'The monarchy exists, not for its own benefit, but for that of the country. We don't come here for our health. We can think of better ways of enjoying ourselves.'

Prince Philip – touring Canada

● 'I owe a lot to my parents, especially my mother and father.'

Golfer Greg Norman

● 'You guys pair up in groups of three, then line up in a circle.'
'Men, I want you just thinking of one word all season. One word and one word only. Super Bowl.'
'You guys have to run a little more than full speed out there.'
'You guys line up alphabetically by height.'

Florida State football coach Bill Peterson

● 'Tragedy is when I cut my finger. Comedy is when you walk into an open sewer and die.'

Actor Mel Brooks

USELESS THINGS PEOPLE SAY

- 'He who hesitates is a damned fool.'

  Mae West

- 'Isn't it a pity that Louis XVI was sent to the scaffold?'

  Prince Philip – to a French Minister

- 'I don't feel we did wrong in taking this great country away from them. There were great numbers of people who needed new land, and the Indians were selfishly trying to keep it to themselves.'

  John Wayne

- 'When I'm a blonde I can say the world is purple, and they'll believe me because they weren't listening to me.'

  Actress Kylie Bax

- 'Everywhere I go I'm asked if I think the university stifles writers. My opinion is that they don't stifle enough of them.'

  US novelist Flannery O'Connor

- 'If you are going through hell, keep going.'

  Sir Winston Churchill

- 'I say no to drugs. But they don't listen.'

  Singer Marilyn Manson

──── USELESS THINGS PEOPLE SAY ────

- 'Now, the only thing that remains unresolved is the resolution of the problem.'

  Ontario State Minister Thomas Wells

- 'It's a pleasant change to be in a country that isn't ruled by its people.'

  Prince Philip – to Paraguay's Dictator

- 'If you, or any member of your family, has been killed, then call us.'

  Orlando TV solicitor's commercial

- 'In the end, we will remember not the words of our enemies, but the silence of our friends.'

  Martin Luther King Jr

- 'The only happy artist is a dead artist, because only then you can't change. After I die, I'll probably come back as a paintbrush.'

  Sylvestor Stallone

- 'Assassins!'

  Italian conductor Arturo Toscanini, speaking to his orchestra

- 'Listen, everyone is entitled to my opinion.'

  Madonna

———— USELESS THINGS PEOPLE SAY ————

• 'We'd like to avoid problems, because when we have problems, we can have troubles.'

Governor Wesley Bolin

• 'I fear the seventh granddaughter and fourteenth grandchild becomes a very uninteresting thing – for it seems to me to go on like rabbits in Windsor Park.'

Queen Victoria

• 'Never refuse an invitation to take the weight off your feet and seize every opportunity you can to relieve yourself.'

King George V's advice to the future King Edward VIII

• 'What does a "No Parking" sign at a certain location mean?'

Multiple-choice question in New York driving test

• 'Too many pieces of music finish too long after the end.'

Igor Stravinsky

• 'If only faces could talk.'

Sportscaster Pat Summerall

• 'She's more royal than the rest of us.'

The Queen – about Princess Michael

——— USELESS THINGS PEOPLE SAY ———

- 'Tom Jones? He's made a million and he's a bloody awful singer.'

  Prince Philip

- 'Sure it's going to kill a lot of people, but they may be dying of something else anyway.'

  Othal Brand – Texas pesticide review board – on chlordane

- 'There are only two tragedies in life: one is not getting what one wants, and the other is getting it.'

  Oscar Wilde

- 'After finding no qualified candidates for the position of principal, the school board is extremely pleased to announce the appointment of David Steele to the post.'

  Rhode Island Superintendent of Schools

- 'My advice to you is get married: if you find a good wife you'll be happy; if not, you'll become a philosopher.'

  Socrates

- 'A verbal contract is not worth the paper it's written on.'

  Samuel Goldwyn

- 'Everything that can be invented has been invented.'

  US Patents Office 1899

USELESS THINGS PEOPLE SAY

- 'My only tangible contribution to British life has been to improve the rear lights on lorries.'
  Prince Philip

- 'He's been around for a while and he's pretty old. He's 35 years old. That will give you some idea of how old he is.'
  Broadcaster Ron Fairley

- 'The President has kept all of the promises he intended to keep.'
  Clinton aide George Stephanopolous

- 'What will you do when you leave football, Jack? Will you stay in football?'
  Stuart Hall, BBC Radio 5

- 'She ought to get a good whipping.'
  Queen Victoria – about a suffragette

- 'I hope to God that he breaks his bloody neck.'
  Prince Philip – about a press cameraman's accident

- 'Traffic is very heavy at the moment, so if you are thinking of leaving now, you'd better set off a few minutes earlier.'
  Dublin radio reporter

——— USELESS THINGS PEOPLE SAY ———

- 'We all get heavier as we get older because there's a lot more information in our heads.'

  Basketball player Vlade Divac

- 'Minks are mean little critters. Vicious, horrible little animals who eat their own. They're not beavers. I'd rather have a mink coat made of mean little critters that are killed in a very nice way and treated nicely for their short, mean lives so that I could keep warm.'

  Actress Valerie Perrine

- 'You know the one thing that's wrong with this country? Everyone gets a chance to have their fair say.'

  US President Bill Clinton

- 'Smoking kills. If you're killed you've lost a very important part of your life.'

  Brooke Shields during anti-smoking campaign

- 'I can't see in this bloody wind.'

  Princess Anne – aged 13 to the Queen

- 'What we have is two important values in conflict. Freedom of speech and our desire for healthy campaigns and a healthy democracy. You can't have both.'

  Missouri representative Dick Gephardt

—— USELESS THINGS PEOPLE SAY ——

- 'Better make it six, I can't eat eight.'
  Baseball player Dan Osinski – when asked how many slices he
  wanted his pizza cut into

- 'His ignorance is encyclopedic.'
  Israeli diplomat and politician Abba Eban

- 'I love California. I practically grew up in Phoenix.'
  US Vice-President Dan Quayle

- 'Which are the monkeys?'
  Prince Philip – confronted by apes and journalists in Gibraltar

- 'Forgive your enemies, but never forget their names.'
  John F Kennedy

- 'Armstrong Jones may be good at something – but it's
  nothing we teach here.'
  Lord Snowdon's school report

- 'The streets are safe in Philadelphia. It's only the people
  who make them unsafe.'
  Ex-Police Chief Frank Rizzo

- 'This is unparalysed in the state's history.'
  Texas Speaker of the House Gib Lewis

—— USELESS THINGS PEOPLE SAY ——

- 'Wishing myself in my sweetheart's arms, whose pretty dukkys I trust shortly to kiss.'

  King Henry VIII – in a letter to Anne Boleyn

- 'If you can't get rid of the skeleton in your closet, you'd best teach it to dance.'

  George Bernard Shaw

- 'There is no housing shortage in Lincoln today. Just a rumour that is put about by people who have nowhere to live.'

  Mayor of Lincoln G L Murfin

- 'A friendship founded on business is better than a business founded on friendship.'

  John D Rockefeller

- 'My father was frightened of his mother. I was frightened of my father. And I am damned well going to see that my children are frightened of me.'

  King George V

- 'You do get fed up with being referred to like a police dog.'

  Prince Charles – on the American tendency to address him simply as 'Prince'

──── USELESS THINGS PEOPLE SAY ────

● 'I have opinions of my own, strong opinions, but I don't always agree with them.'

President George Bush

● 'I would have made a good Pope.'

Richard M Nixon

● 'And now will you all stand and be recognised.'

Texas House Speaker Gib Lewis to crowd in wheelchairs on Disability Day

● 'There are some experiences in life which should not be demanded twice from any man, and one of them is listening to the Brahms *Requiem*.'

George Bernard Shaw

● 'Handsome I cannot think him, with that painfully small and narrow head, those immense features and total want of chin. I never can or shall look at him without a shudder.'

Queen Victoria – on the future King Edward VII

● 'I don't mind praying to the eternal father, but I must be the only man in the country afflicted with an eternal mother.'

The future King Edward VII – about Queen Victoria

——— USELESS THINGS PEOPLE SAY ———

- 'Passive activity income does not include the following income for an activity that is not a passive activity.'
  US Inland Revenue Service form

- 'Whoever designed the streets must have been drunk. I think it was those Irish guys.'
  Minnesota Governor Jesse Ventura

- 'I'm someone who has a deep emotional attachment to *Starsky and Hutch*.'
  US President Bill Clinton

- 'I never left her presence without a sigh of relief.'
  King Edward VII – on Queen Victoria

- 'I've always thought that underpopulated countries in Africa are vastly underpopulated.'
  World Bank chief economist Lawrence Summers

- 'It's the best way of wasting money that I know of.'
  Prince Philip – about the American moon shot

- 'From the moment I picked your book up until I laid it down I was convulsed with laughter. Some day I intend reading it.'
  Groucho Marx

——— USELESS THINGS PEOPLE SAY ———

- 'You dress like a cad. You act like a cad. You are a cad.
  Get out!'
  King George V – to his son, the future King Edward VIII

- 'Facts are stupid things.'
  US President Ronald Reagan

- 'A bachelor's life is no life for a single man.'
  Samuel Goldwyn

- 'The efforts elicited the approbation of the Royal circle.'
  Victorian Court Circular – it meant there was applause

- 'I was provided with additional input that was radically
  different from the truth. I assisted in furthering that
  version.'
  Colonel Oliver North – testifying on Iran-Contra

- 'Man thought hurt but slightly dead.'
  Providence Journal

- 'My presstitutes.'
  Prince Andrew – about journalists

- 'Man shoots neighbour with machete.'
  Miami Herald

──── USELESS THINGS PEOPLE SAY ────

● 'I was under medication when I made the decision to burn the tapes.'

US President Richard Nixon

● 'Being pregnant is the occupational hazard of being a wife.'

Princess Anne

● 'We've got to pause and ask ourselves – how much clean air do we need?'

Ex-Chrysler Chairman Lee Iacocca

● 'Except for his car he's the only man on the track.'
'The lead car is absolutely unique, except for the one behind it, which is identical.'

Sports commentator Murray Walker

● 'You have the mosquitos, we have the press.'

Prince Philip – in the Dominican Republic

● 'If I had a choice of having a woman in my arms or shooting a bad guy on a horse, I'd take the horse. It's a lot more fun.'

Actor Kevin Costner

● 'I am not well. Pray get me a glass of brandy.'

King George IV – in reaction to meeting his arranged bride

———— **USELESS THINGS PEOPLE SAY** ————

● 'I am ready to meet my Maker. Whether my Maker is prepared for the great ordeal of meeting me is another matter.'

Sir Winston Churchill

● 'My favourite pastime is sitting in bed eating chocolates while reading poetry.'

The Queen Mother

● 'False, lying, cowardly, nauseous puppy. The greatest ass, liar and beast in the world.'

King George III – on his eldest son, Prince Frederick

● 'I wish the ground would open up this minute and sink the monster into the lowest hole in hell.'

Queen Caroline – on her eldest son, Prince Frederick

● 'A miserly martinet with an insatiable sexual appetite.'

Prince Frederick – on his father, King George III

● 'Oh doctor, can I have no more fun in bed?'

Queen Victoria – after her doctor's advice to have no more children

● 'A woman can never be too rich or too thin.'

Duchess of Windsor

———— USELESS THINGS PEOPLE SAY ————

- 'He has all the virtues I dislike and none of the vices I admire.'

  Sir Winston Churchill

- 'Marriage is the last decision on which I would want my head to be ruled by my heart.'

  Prince Charles

- 'He slept in long white drawers, which enclosed his feet as well as his legs, like the sleeping suits worn by small babies.'

  Queen Victoria – on Albert's night clothes

- 'He looks like a bell hop at a hotel.'

  Duke of Norfolk – about Lord Snowdon

- 'Sonny Liston has a very unusual injury, a dislocated soldier.'

  Boxer Henry Cooper, on the BBC

- 'His previous wives just didn't understand him.'

  Mickey Rooney's eighth wife, Jan Chamberlein

- 'The world is more like it is now than it ever was before.'

  US President Dwight D Eisenhower

──────── # USELESS THINGS PEOPLE SAY ────────

- 'I won't knight buggers.'

  King George V – about homosexuals

- 'This country makes me gasp – and it isn't just the altitude.'

  Princess Alexandra – on Mexico

- 'I did not realise I could really hate people as I do the Germans, though I never liked them.'

  Queen Mary, 1941

- 'Every drop of blood in my veins is German.'

  King Edward VIII

- 'If we don't succeed we run the risk of failure.'
  'It is wonderful to be here in the great state of Chicago.'
  'Illegitimacy is something we should talk about in terms of not having.'
  'It's time for the human race to enter the solar system.'
  'It isn't pollution that is hurting the environment, it's the impurities in our air and water that are doing it.'
  'What a waste it is to lose one's mind. Or not to have a mind is being very wasteful. How true that is.'

  US Vice-President Dan Quayle

- 'It was more like being kidnapped.'

  Princess Margaret – on her visit to Morocco

—— USELESS THINGS PEOPLE SAY ——

● 'I cannot tell you how grateful I am – I am filled with humidity.'

Speaker of the House Gib Lewis

● 'The places where I need work are on my inside and outside games.'

Basketball player Darnell Hillman

● 'There is only one Jesus Christ. All the rest is a dispute over trifles.'

Queen Elizabeth I – on religion

● 'You can get used to anyone's face in a week.'

King Charles II – about his new bride

● 'We are trying to change the 1974 Constitution, whenever that was passed.'

Louisiana State Representative Donald Kennard

● 'I haven't committed a crime. All I did was fail to comply with the law.'

New York Mayor David Dinkins – on failing to pay taxes

● 'Any time Detroit scores more than 100 points and holds the other team below 100 points they almost always win.'

Basketball commentator Doug Collins

——— USELESS THINGS PEOPLE SAY ———

- 'Lack of brains hinders research.'

  Columbus Dispatch

- 'He will be known for a long time because of me.'

  Duchess of Windsor – about the Duke

- 'We are unable to announce the weather. We depend on
  weather reports from the airport, which is closed, due to
  weather. Whether we will be able to give you a weather
  report tomorrow will depend on the weather.'

  Arab news report

- 'Where the hell is Australia, anyway?'

  Singer Britney Spears

- 'I didn't know "Onward Christian Soldiers" was a
  Christian song.'

  Texas politician Aggie Pate

- 'I have a God-given talent. I got it from my dad.'

  Missouri sportsman Julian Wakefield

- 'He's passé. Nobody cares about Mickey any more. There
  are whole batches of Mickeys we just can't give away. I
  think we should phase him out!'

  Roy Disney to brother Walt, 1937

———— USELESS THINGS PEOPLE SAY ————

- 'What did you do about peeing?'

  King George V – to Charles Lindbergh after
  he flew the Atlantic solo

- 'I love Mickey Mouse more than any woman I have ever known.'

  Walt Disney

- 'These people haven't seen the last of my face. If I go down, I'm going down standing up.'

  Basketball player Chuck Person

- 'The Supreme Court rules that murderers shall not be electrocuted twice for the same crime.'

  Cleveland Daily News headline

- 'Not everything that can be counted counts, and not everything that counts can be counted.'

  Albert Einstein

LITERATURE
AND ART

LITERATURE AND ART

- In the book *Gone With the Wind*, Melanie's pregnancy lasts 21 months – based on the actual battles mentioned.

- Madrid's Prado Art Museum is named after the fields that once surrounded it. Meadow, in Spanish, is *prado*.

- James Joyce chose the date on which his novel *Ulysses*, takes place in Dublin – 16 June 1904 – after the day on which he had his first date with his future wife, Nora Barnacle.

- Author Ian Fleming gave the name James Bond to his spy hero after seeing it on the cover of a book of West Indian birds, by ornithologist James Bond.

- Jules Verne, who wrote about amazing voyages to the moon and around the earth, only ever went aloft in a machine once – a balloon ascent in 1873.

- When asked to name his favourite among all his paintings Pablo Picasso replied 'the next one'.

- Mick Jagger turned down a £3.5 million advance offer on his memoirs from a publisher because, he said, he 'couldn't remember' enough significant details from his own life.

LITERATURE AND ART

- The part of Hamlet, by William Shakespeare, is the longest of the playwright's speaking parts with 1,530 lines. The second longest part is that of Richard III with 1,164 lines.

- A book published in 1940 contained 370 proofs of the Pythagorean theorem, including one by former US President James Garfield.

- The measurement of one foot is based on a third of the length of the arm of King Henry I of England.

- Alexandra Dumas named his palatial home in Paris 'Monte Christo' after his most famous novel, *The Count of Monte Christo*.

- Agatha Christie claimed she did most of the plotting for her detective stories while sitting in a bath tub eating apples.

- Hypersonic is five times the speed of sound.

- When a speaker accidentally transposes the initial sounds or letters of two or more words, often to humorous effect, it is called a spoonerism. For example, saying Jag of Flapan instead of Flag of Japan.

———————— LITERATURE AND ART ————————

- Pulitzer Prize-winner William Faulkner once worked as a rum runner to make money because he couldn't find a publisher to print his novels.

- Disney cleaned up the story of *Snow White and the Seven Dwarfs* for his feature cartoon. In the original Grimm Brothers fairytale the Queen was condemned to dance in red-hot iron shoes until she died. Disney had her falling of a precipice to her death.

- There was room for 150 knights around King Arthur's famous round table.

- It was a combination of the two words 'will comply' that produced the radio-code response 'wilco'.

- For a short time in 1967 the American Typers' Association made a new punctuation mark called an interrobang, which was a combination of the question mark and an exclamation mark. It was rarely used and hasn't been seen since.

- John Le Carré's real name is David John Moore Cornwell.

- Gambrinous is a word meaning being full of beer.

———————— LITERATURE AND ART ————————

- Author Lewis Carroll combined the words 'chuckle' and 'snort' to come up with the word 'chortle' in *Through the Looking Glass.*

- Oology is the study or collecting of birds' eggs.

- Elizabeth Barrett Browning's pet cocker spaniel was called Flush.

- Transurphobia is the fear of haircuts.

- Painter Jocopo Robusti became far better known by his nickname, 'Little Dyer' or 'Tintorette'. His father was a silk-dyer.

- Dylan Thomas once unkindly pointed out that, except for one misplaced letter, T S Eliot's name spelled backwards is 'Toilets'.

- The father of Geoffrey Chaucer, who wrote the *Canterbury Tales*, was a London wine merchant.

- The first names of Dr Jekyll and Mr Hyde were Henry and Edward.

- Dr Frankenstein's first name was Victor.

LITERATURE AND ART

- The Declaration of Independence was written on hemp paper.

- 'Able was I ere I saw Elba' is a palindrome written by Napoleon.

- Robinson Crusoe was marooned on his desert island for 24 years.

- One edition of the current *Sunday New York Times* has more information in it than a typical adult was exposed to in an entire lifetime a hundred years ago.

- The slow-witted character named Moron in Molière's play *La Princesse d'Elide* created a new word in the dictionary.

- Robin Hood's friend, Little John, was really called John Little.

- The International Association of Women Helicopter Pilots is known as the Whirly Girls.

- The only novel to top the best-sellers' list for two consecutive years – 1972 and 1973 – was Richard Bach's *Jonathan Livingstone Seagull*.

─────── LITERATURE AND ART ───────

- Ezra Pound, William Joyce and P G Wodehouse all made broadcasts for the enemy during World War II.

- In 1900 Americans voted their favourite book, after the Bible, as *The Sears Roebuck Catalogue.*

- Salvador Dali's wife was the model for the Christ figure in Dali's painting *The Sacrament of the Last Supper.*

- The pasta vermicelli means 'little worms'.

- The letter 'w' is the only letter in the alphabet that does not have just one syllable. It has three.

- Charles Dickens penned in Puny Pete, Little Larry and Small Sam before settling on Tiny Tim for his crippled child in *A Christmas Carol.*

- The sitter in Leonardo da Vinci's *Mona Lisa* has no eyebrows.

- Oscar Wilde once remarked that, 'America was often discovered before Columbus, but it was always hushed up.'

- The term 'maverick' came from Texas rancher Sam Maverick, who refused to brand his calves.

LITERATURE AND ART

- The line 'Three quarks for Muster Mark!' in James Joyce's *Ulysses* provided the name for the subatomic particles now known as 'quarks', named by physicist Murray Gell-Mann.

- The first book manuscript to be typed before being sent to a publisher was Mark Twain's *The Adventures of Tom Sawyer* in 1876 – when the first typewriter was manufactured.

- The 'y' in old words like 'ye' is better pronounced with a 'th' sound and not a 'y' sound. In Latin the 'th' sound did not exist and the Romans occupying England used the rune 'thorne' to represent the 'th' sounds. When the printing presses were invented the character from the Roman alphabet which most closely resembled the 'thorne' was the lower case 'y'.

- The phrase 'United we stand, divided we fall' was first used in the Aesop fable *The Four Oxen and the Lion*, written nearly 600 years before Christ.

- The children's poem *The Pied Piper of Hamlyn* was written by Robert Browning.

- Charles Dickens took just six weeks to write *A Christmas Carol*.

──────── **LITERATURE AND ART** ────────

● The opposite end of a hammer to the striking end is called the peen.

● The highest scoring three-letter word in Scrabble is Zax, which is a tool for cutting and trimming roof slates.

● The letters of the word 'SHAZAM', which was shouted to conjure up comic-book hero Captain Marvel, stood for Solomon's Wisdom, Hercules's Strength, Atlas's Stamina, Zeus's Power, Achilles's Courage and Mercury's Speed.

● The first name of Jeeves, the fictional butler created by P G Woodhouse in 1915, remained a mystery for many years (even to his employer). It was later revealed in her 1971 novel *Much Obliged Jeeves*. His name was Reginald.

● A trilemma is a dilemma with a third alternative.

● The single dot over the lower-case letter 'i' is called a tipple.

● The most commonly used word in English conversation is 'I'.

● There are twenty different kinds of kisses described in the erotic Indian text the *Kama Sutra*.

LITERATURE AND ART

- The writer Edgar Allen Poe and singer Jerry Lee Lewis both married their thirteen-year-old cousins.

- Popeye the sailorman's home port was called Sweetwater.

- The first time Goofy appeared in a Mickey Mouse cartoon he was known as Dippy Dawg. He was renamed in the 1930s when he began to star regularly with Mickey.

- In the US strip cartoon *Blondie* Dagwood once remarked: 'The trouble with the rat race is that there is never a finish line.'

- The Aboriginal word 'koala' means 'no drink'. The Australian creature gets all its liquid and food from eucalyptus leaves.

- The Grand Vizier of Persia in the tenth century, Abdul Kassan Ismael, took his library with him wherever he went. The 117,000 volumes of books were carried by 400 camels trained to walk in alphabetical order.

- The only word in the English language that both begins and ends with the letters 'und' is 'underground'.

——————— LITERATURE AND ART ———————

- Dr Watson's bullet wound moved according to different Sherlock Holmes stories. In *A Study in Scarle* it was in his shoulder but in *The Sign of Four* it was in his leg.

- Edgar Allen Poe was expelled from West Point Military Academy for turning out on a public parade wearing only his white belt and gloves.

- One seven-letter word that contains ten other words without any of the letters being rearranged is 'therein'. It includes 'the', 'there', 'he', 'in', 'rein', 'her', 'here', 'ere', 'therein' and 'herein'.

- During World War I Agatha Christie worked in a hospital dispensary and it is there she acquired her extensive knowledge of poisons.

- In ancient Greece writing had no space between the words.

- The first complete bible printed in the United States was in the language of the Algonquian Indians. It was translated and published in 1663 by the Reverend John Eliot.

- In most of the world's languages the word for mother begins with the letter 'M'.

LITERATURE AND ART

- In Africa the house of the wicked witch in *Hansel and Gretel* is not made of gingerbread but of salt – which is highly prized by children.

- Each of the sunflowers in Vincent Van Gogh's painting *Sunflowers* sold at auction in 1987, was worth $2.66 million. There are fifteen in the painting.

- 'Strengths' is the longest word in the English language with just one vowel.

- During World War II there were two types of dirigibles – the A-rigid and the B-limp. The second became the common-usage name for a dirigible – blimp.

- Ernest Hemingway once admitted that he had revised the last page of *A Farewell to Arms* 39 times.

- The name of the female ape that became Tarzan's foster mother was Kala.

- The Nepalese word for the Abominable Snowman is *Metohkangmi*, which means 'the indescribably filthy man of the snow'.

- Rembrandt's last name was van Ryn.

—————— LITERATURE AND ART ——————

- The first person who referred to a coward as a chicken was William Shakespeare.

- The word 'monosyllable' has five syllables.

- A vexillologist studies flags.

- The Australian slang term 'hooloo' means goodbye.

- Virginia Woolf wrote all her books standing up.

- The Japanese word 'judo' means 'the gentle way'.

- The original meaning of the word 'clue' was a ball of thread or yarn. Like its modern namesake, it often took some time to unravel.

- Medieval ecclesiastical calendars had the important saints and feast days highlighted in red ink. These memorable days became known as 'red-letter days'.

- Mark Twain failed to graduate from elementary school.

- The longest sentence in literature was written by Victor Hugo in *Les Misérables* and came to a staggering 823 words.

LITERATURE AND ART

- In olden days the top crust of a loaf of bread would always be presented to the king, or highest-ranking person, at the table. Hence the expression 'upper crust' for high-ranking people.

- In the Batman stories the Riddler's real name was Edward or E Nigma.

- Ian Fleming's favourite cocktail was Pink Gin and not that of his spy hero, James Bond – a Vodka Martini.

- Oscar Wilde lived out the last three years of his life in France as Sebastian Melmoth.

- An American billion is 1,000 million – a British billion is 1,000,000 million.

- The full medical description of a black eye is 'bilateral perorbital haematoma'.

- Long before Lois Lane came along, the high-school sweetheart of Superman's alter ego was Lana Lang.

- 'Queuetopia' was a word invented by Winston Churchill to describe communist countries where people had to line up to buy anything.

———————— LITERATURE AND ART ————————

- A nineteenth-century advertisement for a McCoy sewing machine introduced the phrase 'The real McCoy' into the English language.

- Sherlock Holmes was known as Sherringford Holmes in the first short story written by Sir Arthur Conan Doyle in 1886. His side-kick was then called Ormond Sacker, who would later evolve into Thomas Watson.

- The word 'spam' is an acronym formed from SPiced hAM.

- The next-door neighbours of Miss Marple in St Mary Mead village were Dr Haydock and Miss Harnell.

- A duffle bag is so called because the thick wool originally used to make the bags came from the Belgium town of Duffle.

- Casanova named 116 lovers in his memoirs *The Story of my Life,* even though he often boasted of seducing thousands.

- In artist Emanuel Leutze's famous 1851 painting *Washington Crossing the Delaware* he used the Rhine in his native Germany.

—————————LITERATURE AND ART—————————

- Arthur Conan Doyle was awarded a knighthood for his defence of the British concentration camps during the Boer Wars and not because of his Sherlock Holmes stories.

- In Victorian times Goldilocks, of *Three Bears* fame, was known as Silver Hair. She later became Golden Hair and eventually Goldilocks.

- The difference between a nook and a cranny is that the nook is a corner and the cranny is a crack.

- The American State Department refers to elevators as 'vertical transportation units'.

- In the native Greek Utopia means 'not a place' or 'nowhere'.

- Race car is a palindrome.

- The only mention of the United States of America by Shakespeare was in his play *The Comedy of Errors*.

- Shakespeare's daughters were called Susanna and Judith.

- Rip Van Winkle's dog was called Victor.

LITERATURE AND ART

- It was US critic, author and poet Dorothy Parker who wrote 'Men don't make passes at girls who wear glasses.'

- The word 'robot' comes from the Czechoslovakian word '*robotovat*', which means to work very hard. It was created by Karel Capek.

- The phrase 'passing the buck' comes from the old American custom of using a buckhorn-handled knife, placed in front of the dealer during a game of cards. A player who didn't want the deal would pass the knife, or buckhorn, to the next player.

- John Steinbeck worked as a hod carrier, conveying concrete along scaffolding during the construction of New York's Madison Square Garden in the 1930s.

- Playwright Tom Stoppard's native language is Czechoslovakian. His Czech mother married an English army officer named Stoppard.

- The word 'moose' comes from the Algonquian Indian language.

- Eosophobia is a fear of the dawn.

──────────── LITERATURE AND ART ────────────

- According to Ernest Hemingway four achievements are necessary to become a real man. You should plant a tree, fight a bull, write a book and have a son.

- The shortest French word with all five vowels is '*oiseau*' meaning bird.

- The term 'strike' originated in 1768 when British sailors refused to work and showed this by striking, or lowering, the sails on their ships.

- Sir Arthur Conan Doyle was paid £25 for his first published story about Sherlock Holmes, *A Study in Scarlet*, which appeared in *Beeton's Christmas Annual* in 1887.

- Halley's Comet came into view in 1835 when Mark Twain was born, and was again in view in 1910 when he died.

- Isaac Asimov is the only author to have a book in every Dewey decimal category.

- The letters HIOX in the Latin alphabet are the only ones that look the same if you turn them upside down or see them from behind.

——————— **LITERATURE AND ART** ———————

- The J R R initials in Tolkien's name stand for John Ronald Reuel.

- The English word 'indivisibility' has only one vowel that occurs six times.

- The only word in English that consists of two letters, used three times, is 'deeded'.

- 'Facetiously' and 'abstemiously' are the only two words in the English language that contain all the vowels, including 'y', in alphabetical order.

- Only two of the Sherlock Holmes stories are written with him as the narrator. They are *The Blanched Soldier* and *The Lion's Mane*.

- The only Dutch word to contain eight consecutive consonants is *angstschreeuw*.

- The English syllable 'ough' can be pronounced nine different ways. One sentence that contains them all is: 'A rough-coated, dough-faced thoughtful ploughman strode through the streets of Scarborough and after falling into his slough he coughed and hiccoughed.'

LITERATURE AND ART

- Left-handed people cannot write Mandarin Chinese.

- The contraction of the Middle Ages phrase 'God be with ye' produced the modern word 'goodbye'.

- 'Dreamt' is the only English word that ends in the letters 'mt'.

PEOPLE
POINTERS

PEOPLE POINTERS

- To thank actor Harrison Ford for narrating a documentary, the London Museum of Natural History named a spider after him called *Calponia Harrisonfordi*.

- The only president to be head of a labour union was Ronald Reagan.

- When Einstein was inducted as an American citizen he went to the ceremony with no socks on.

- In the shower 75% of people wash from their tops to their bottoms.

- The world's tallest woman, Zeng Jinlian, from China, was 8 feet 1 ¾ inches (2 m 4.5 cm) tall.

- Oliver Cromwell was exhumed, hanged and decapitated two years after he died.

- Neil Armstrong stepped on to the moon using his left foot first.

- The only woman in history to have married both a king of France and a king of England was Eleanor of Aquitane. Her husbands were Louis VII of France and Henry II of England.

To Dad,

With lots of love and

huge Christmas cuddles,

Lorna

xxxx

PEOPLE POINTERS

- The last Ranee of Sarawak, who selected mistresses for her husband, the Raja, boasted that he had only ever rejected one of her choices.

- Attila the Hun died of a nosebleed on his wedding night in AD 453.

- The 'new' bridal extra, which Wallis Simpson wore to her wedding with Edward VIII, was a gold coin, which she carried in her left shoe. It had been minted for Edward's coronation.

- In a lifetime the average person spends eighteen months on the telephone.

- Fleet commanders in the Pacific Theatre of war in World War II, Admiral Isoroku Yamamoto for the Japanese and Admiral Chester Nimitz for the United States, were each missing two fingers as a result of accidents while young officers on board ship.

- Fresca, a grapefruit-flavoured soda sold on the east coast of America, was liked so much by US President Lyndon Johnson that he had a fountain installed in the Oval Office that dispensed the drink. He operated the soda fountain by pushing a button on his desk chair.

PEOPLE POINTERS

- William Wrigley gave away free packs of chewing gum to customers who bought his baking powder. He soon abandoned the baking powder when he discovered they were buying it in order to get his gum.

- President Lyndon Johnson had an aunt named Frank.

- The word 'feminism' was misspelled 'feminisim' on the May/June 1996 cover of *Ms Magazine*.

- Half of all Americans live within 50 miles (80.46 km) of where they grow up.

- John Wilkes Booth shot President Lincoln in a theatre and was found in a warehouse. Lee Harvey Oswald shot President Kennedy from a warehouse and was found in a theatre.

- The only US president to remain a bachelor was James Buchanon.

- The Red Baron's real name was Manfred von Richthofen.

- The world's first popular elected female head of state was Sirimauo Bandranaike of Sri Lanka, in 1960.

PEOPLE POINTERS

- Cleopatra used squeezed pomegranate seeds for lipstick

- On his way to the South Sea islands, French painter Paul Gauguin stopped off briefly in Central America, where he worked as a labourer on the Panama Canal.

- The Scottish name Campbell actually means 'crooked mouth' in Gaelic.

- US President Theodore Roosevelt's wife and mother both died on the same day.

- Orson Welles is buried in an olive grove in Seville, Spain, owned by his friend and matador Antonio Ordonez.

- In the wall paintings ancient Etruscans used to decorate tombs, they painted women white and men red.

- Teddy Roosevelt was so keen on boxing he had a boxing ring installed in the White House.

- Stalin, whose left arm was noticeably shorter than his right, also had webbed toes on his left foot.

- Some American Indians did not eat turkey meat because they believed killing such a timid bird showed laziness.

PEOPLE POINTERS

- The most common name in the world is Mohammed.

- Communist guru Leon Trotsky was killed in Mexico with an ice pick. It entered his skull and became wedged in his brain. His assassin had to struggle with Trotsky to remove it, in order to hit him a second time!

- Everybody's tongue print is unique.

- To celebrate his 700th parachute jump Flight Sergeant Hector Macmillan made his descent in full national Scottish dress while playing 'The Road to the Isles' on the bagpipes.

- The most common name in Italy is Mario Rossi.

- Alexander the Great was an epileptic.

- People become sick a great deal more by staying indoors than by going out in the cold.

- Ronald Reagan was the oldest man to be elected president of the United States.

- There are more psychoanalysts in Buenos Aires, Argentina, than in any other city in the world.

PEOPLE POINTERS

- The car-making Dodge brothers, Horace and John, were Jewish, which is why the first Dodge emblem had a Star of David in it.

- Confucius was the eleventh child of a 70-year-old soldier.

- Richard Millhouse Nixon's name contains all the letters from the word 'criminal'. He was the first US president to have this distinction. The second was William Jefferson Clinton.

- The youngest pope was only eleven years old.

- US President Lyndon Johnson's family all shared the initials 'LBJ'. They were: Lyndon Baines Johnson, Lady Bird Johnson, Linda Bird Johnson and Lucy Baines Johnson. His dog was Little Beagle Johnson.

- For his world-first transatlantic flight, pilot Charles Lindberg took only four sandwiches for food.

- During American conscription for World War II there were nine recorded cases of men having three testicles.

- Marco Polo was born on the Croatian Island of Korcula.

PEOPLE POINTERS

- For religious reasons Franklin Pierce was the only US president to say 'I promise' instead of 'I swear' at his inauguration.

- Every American president since World War II who addressed the Canadian House of Commons during his first term of office went on to be re-elected for a second term – Eisenhower, Nixon, Reagan and Clinton. Kennedy, Johnson, Ford, Carter and Bush, who did not address the Parliament, did not win a second term.

- While painting a mural around the rim of the US Capitol artist Constantino Brumidi fell from the dome. He died four months later.

- Wartime President Franklin D Roosevelt was the first to have a presidential aircraft. He only flew on the specially equipped Douglas DC4, nicknamed 'the sacred cow', once – to travel to Yalta for the conference with Stalin and Churchill. The plane was fitted with a lift so he could board it in his wheelchair.

- Actor Laurence Oliver – later Lord Olivier – once called a press conference just to complain about service on British Rail. He was furious that kippers had been dropped from the menu.

PEOPLE POINTERS

- Lee Harvey Oswald was dyslexic.

- Picasso's full name was Pablo Diego Jose Francisco de Paula Juan Nepomuceno Maria de los Remedios Cipriano de la Santisima Trinidad Ruiz Picasso.

- More than 200 people in West Virginia returned their licence plates to the Motor Vehicle Bureau because they began with the letters 'OJ'.

- A survey of career women who chose tattoos revealed that they preferred to adorn their left breast rather than their right breast by a ratio of three to one.

- As the result of a duel being fought before becoming president, Andrew Jackson spent his adult life with a bullet no more than two inches (5 cm) away from his heart.

- The dog that shared the bed of Napoleon and Josephine was called Fortune.

- At night the average person is about a quarter of an inch (0.6 cm) taller.

- Jimmy Carter was the first US president to have been born in a hospital.

PEOPLE POINTERS

- Of the 102 people on board the *Mayflower* ten of them were called John.

- In the Philippines the yo-yo was originally used as a weapon.

- Henry Ford never had a driving licence.

- The voice on the AOL e-mail service that says 'Hello', 'You've got mail' and 'Goodbye' is that of Elwood Elridge, a company employee.

- Before he discovered his real vocation as a lover and libertine, Casanova was preparing for the priesthood.

- US President Andrew Jackson's pet parrot had to be removed from his funeral in 1845 because it was swearing.

- Vincent van Gogh committed suicide while painting *Wheat Field with Crows*.

- US President John F Kennedy's rocking chair fetched $443,000 at auction.

- King Louis XIV reigned for 72 years. He acceded to the throne at the age of five in 1643. He once declared: 'L'Etat? C'est moi' – I am the State.

PEOPLE POINTERS

- Ian Lewis of Standish, Lancashire, England, spent 30 years tracing his family history and contacting 2,000 distant relatives before discovering he was adopted as a one-month-old baby.

- Only one person in two billion will live to be 116 years old or over.

- Physicist Stephen Hawking was given just two years to live at the age of 21. On 8 January 2003 he was 61.

- Somdetch Thra Paramendr Naha Mongkut was otherwise known as the King of Siam – the 'King and I' immortalised by writer Margaret Langden.

- US President Gerald Ford was once a male model.

- The only US president to win a Pulitzer Prize was John F Kennedy for his biography *Profiles in Courage*.

- Elizabeth I of England suffered from anthophobia – a fear of roses.

- Humans spend almost a third of their lives in bed.

- Captain Kidd named his ship *The Adventure Galley*.

PEOPLE POINTERS

- When asked what he thought of Western civilisation, Mahatma Gandhi replied: 'I think it would be a good idea.'

- After the death of Chaim Weizmann in 1952 the presidency of Israel was offered to Albert Einstein – who turned it down.

- The Roman emperor Nero, whose father was dead and mother in exile, was brought up by a barber and a male ballet dancer.

- Abraham Lincoln's mother died after drinking milk from the family cow, which had eaten poisonous mushrooms.

- The Greek national anthem has 158 verses. No one in Greece has memorised all of them.

- Stalin's real name was Iosif Vissarionovich Dzhugashvili. He began using the pseudonym Stalin, meaning 'Man of Steel', in 1936.

- Helen of Troy was Queen of Sparta.

- The scientist Sir Isaac Newton was a fully ordained priest in the Church of England.

PEOPLE POINTERS

- Two presidential families had their own way of preventing their conversations being overheard by White House guests or staff. The Hoovers spoke to each other in Chinese. The Coolidge family spoke in sign language.

- The average person is said to have 1,460 dreams a year.

- The famous scar that earned Al Capone his nickname of 'Scarface' was inflicted by the brother of a girl he had insulted. The boy attacked him with a knife leaving him with the three distinctive scars.

- Because snow is relatively unknown on the continent of Africa, children there know the fairytale heroine as 'Flower White' rather than as Snow White.

- Women in New Zealand were the first in the world to be given the vote – in 1890.

- Mexican revolutionary Sancho Villa's dying words were: 'Don't let it end like this. Tell them I said something.'

- People start to shrink after the age of 30.

- The average man can read smaller print than the average woman.

PEOPLE POINTERS

- Women can hear better than men can.

- When George Washington was US President there were only some 350 federal employees.

- There were six rulers of Egypt named Cleopatra before the woman who became linked with Julius Caesar and Mark Anthony.

- Winston Churchill was born in a ladies' room during a dance.

- French statesman Cardinal Richelieu would jump over the furniture every morning as his daily exercise routine.

- Most people button their shirts upwards.

- Sir Walter Raleigh had a black greyhound called Hamlet.
- By law, every Swiss citizen is required to have a bomb shelter or access to a bomb shelter.

- Guru of psychology Sigmund Freud had a morbid fear of ferns.

- The world's tallest man was an American, Robert Wadlo, who was eight feet eleven inches tall.

PEOPLE POINTERS

- Genghis Khan's first job was as a goatherd.

- 'Speak of the devil' is a shortened version of 'Speak of the devil and he shall come.' It was believed that if you spoke about the devil, it would attract his attention. That is why the phrase is used when a person appears just after being mentioned.

- Queen Victoria had a sprig of holly placed below her collar as a child to train her to keep her chin up.

- Both Napoleon and Hitler had only one testicle.

- The Prince of Wales, later to become Edward VIII, was saved from arrest during a police Prohibition raid by singer Texas Guinan, who pushed him into her nightclub kitchen and gave him a chef's hat and skillet.

- The Declaration of Independence was signed by only two people – John Hancock and Charles Thomson – on the first Independence Day, 4 July 1776. Most added their signatures on 2 August, but the last was not appended until five years later.

- Someone who is concerned with the quadrature of a circle is called a tetragondzein.

PEOPLE POINTERS

- When evidence to decide whether a person should be sanctified is brought before the Vatican judges in a Catholic court, a devil's advocate is always appointed to give the alternative view.

- After Egypt's King Farouk was overthrown by Gamal Nasser, he predicted that one day there would be only five kings left in the world – the kings of Hearts, Spades, Diamonds, Clubs and England.

- Richard Nixon's favourite drink was a dry Martini.

- According to its state constitution, in Arizona every male over the age of eighteen is considered to be part of the State Militia.

- Beau Brummell's real name was George.

- Until nearly a hundred years ago nearly all people in Martha's Vineyard – a resort island off the coast of Massachusetts, to the south of Cape Cod – were bilingual in sign language and English. It developed its own dialect of sign language when a deaf person arrived in 1692. Between then and 1910 the relatively large, genetically deaf population, and most other inhabitants, recognised and could use their own particular sign language.

PEOPLE POINTERS

- Abraham Lincoln was the only president to be awarded a patent – for a device to lift boats over shoals without discharging their cargo.

- Children grow faster in springtime than at any other time of year.

- Captain William Bligh, of the *Mutiny on the Bounty* fame, was thrown out after another mutiny almost 20 years after that event. While he was governor of New South Wales, in 1808, British army officers captured him and forced him to resign. He had tried to stop the colony's rum trade.

- In 1946, to celebrate Aga Khan's 60 years as leader of the Ismaili Sect of the Shiite Muslims, his followers gave his weight in diamonds. He weighed 243¼ lb (111 kg).

- The girl in the Statue of Liberty is called 'Mother of Exiles'.

- Queen Anne's bow legs inspired a furniture style.

- Over 40 years Herbert Hoover gave all his political earnings to charity, including his wages and pension as US president.

--------------------- **PEOPLE POINTERS** ---------------------

- The world's youngest parents lived in China, in 1910, and were eight and nine years of age.

- The first president to ride in an automobile was William McKinley, after he was shot. He was taken to hospital in a 1901 Columbia electric ambulance.

- In his various palaces the French King Louis XIV had 413 beds.

- Sarah Delano Roosevelt never learned to entrust her son with the management of the family's financial affairs and never thought he was up to the task – even though Franklin D presided over eight annual budgets of the largest fiscal entity on earth: the United States.

- King Prajadhipok, the ruler of Siam, took out insurance with French and British insurance companies against unemployment. He collected and lived comfortably on the proceeds in England for six years, after which time he was overthrown in the early 1930s.

- During his time as president William Taft had a bathtub big enough to hold four normal men installed in the White House in order to accommodate his massive 23-stone (146.06-kg) figure.

PEOPLE POINTERS

- Violet Gibson Burns typed continuously at her typewriter for 264 hours – a world record.

- England's King Henry VI was only nine months old when he acceded to the throne.

- James Monroe ran unopposed for his second term in the presidency in 1820. The only other candidate to have run unopposed was George Washington.

- In 1990/91 *Who's Who in America* carried ten lines about Ronald Reagan – and 28 lines about his wife, Nancy.

- When Imelda Marcos and her deposed Filipino husband, President Ferdinand Marcos, went into exile in 1986, she left behind 2,400 pairs of size 8 ½ shoes.

- In the eight-year period Ronald Reagan was president, the White House bought 12 tons of his favourite jelly beans.

- Every night Cleopatra had her mattress stuffed with rose petals.

- Theodore Roosevelt was the only president not to use the word 'I' in his inaugural address.

PEOPLE POINTERS

- Lyndon Johnson was obsessed with secrecy. He usually wrote 'burn this', even on his personal mail.

- U Thant was Secretary General to the United Nations until 1971. His name means 'Mr Clean' in English.

- During the eleven-month-long African hunting expedition that followed Theodore Roosevelt's term as president in 1909, he shot 296 animals including nine lions and five elephants.

- Eight of America's presidents were born British subjects.

- President Lyndon Johnson called his pet beagles Him and Her. President Franklin D Roosevelt and wife Eleanor called their pistols, which they kept under their pillows, His and Hers.

- Before founding the Russian communist party and becoming Premier of the first Soviet Government, Lenin lived in exile in England, under the name of Jacob Richter.

- James Madison was the smallest president in US history, measuring just five feet four inches and weighing just seven stone.

PEOPLE POINTERS

- Joan of Arc was only nineteen years of age when she was burned at the stake.

- George Washington named his three foxhounds Drunkard, Tippler and Tipsy.

- Cleopatra was only twelve years old when she took her first lover.

- English haberdasher James Hetherington was arrested in 1797 when he wore a silk top hat for the first time in London. The charge read that he was guilty of wearing a 'tall structure of shining lustre calculated to disturb the people'.

- George Washington's second inaugural address was the shortest in history and contained only 135 words.

- Romans had three words to describe kisses: the kiss for acquaintances, the *basium*; the kiss between close friends, the *osculum*; and the kiss between lovers, the *suavium*.

- When President Lincoln's widow Mary Todd Lincoln was declared insane in 1875, doctors found $56,000 worth of bonds concealed in her underwear.

PEOPLE POINTERS

- Polar explorer Admiral Byrd's dog was called Igloo.

- Ulyses S Grant was booked for speeding in Washington during his term as president. He was driving a horse and buggy – and was fined $5.

- In 1512 Louis XII of France ordered the removal of all the garbage, which for years had been routinely thrown over the walls of Paris. He did it not for hygienic reasons, but because an enemy might scale the garbage to climb over the walls.

- The Kwakiutl Indians earned more admiration from their fellows for destroying possessions than for accumulating them.

- The average clerk produces 4.6 lb (2 kg) of waste paper a day.

- The Irish Baron of Kinsale has the privilege of retaining his hat in the presence of royalty.

- Men experience higher blood pressure during orgasm than women do.

- More than half the world's population still rely on their own or their animals' muscles for all their power.

PEOPLE POINTERS

- The fashion of women having their nipples pierced to wear gold or jewelled pins or rings is not a new one. It began in England around 1890.

- In 1841 in England a third of the men and half the women who married signed the register with a mark rather than their written names.

- More people play the bagpipes today than at any time in history.

- The first English royal to wear a pair of silk stockings was a man – King Henry VIII, in 1509. The stockings were a gift from Spain.

- Cambridge students were not allowed to keep dogs in their rooms. Lord Byron kept a bear.

- In the Masters and Johnson study the man with the longest penis was just five feet seven inches tall.

- Louis XIV France took only three baths during his 77-year lifetime: one when he was baptised; one at the insistence of one of his mistresses; and the last when a doctor lanced a boil on his bottom and ordered him to soak it in a tub of hot water.

—————— PEOPLE POINTERS ——————

- In the early days of Hollywood, western sets were made to seven-eighths scale to make the heroes seem larger.

SEVENS

SEVENS

- *The Magnificent Seven*
  Charles Bronson – Bernordo
  Yul Brynner – Chris
  Horst Buchholz – Chico
  James Coburn – Britt
  Brad Dexter – Harry
  Steve McQueen – Vin
  Robert Vaughn – Lee

- The Seven Dwarfs
  Bashful
  Doc
  Dopey
  Grumpy
  Happy
  Sleepy
  Sneezy

- The Seven Deadly Sins
  Avarice
  Envy
  Gluttony
  Lust
  Pride
  Sloth
  Wrath

SEVENS

- The Seven Wonders of the Ancient World
  Pyramids of Giza
  Hanging Gardens of Babylon
  Mausoleum of Halicarnassus
  Temple of Artemis at Ephesus
  Colossus of Rhodes
  Pharos (Lighthouse) of Alexandria
  Statue of Zeus at Olympia

- The Seven Virtues
  Justice
  Fortitude
  Prudence
  Temperance
  Faith
  Hope
  Charity

- The Seven Seas
  North Atlantic Ocean
  South Atlantic Ocean
  North Pacific Ocean
  South Pacific Ocean
  Indian Ocean
  Arctic Ocean
  Antarctic Ocean

---------------------------- **SEVENS** ----------------------------

- The Seven Sizes of Grand Piano
  Baby Grand – 5 ft 8 inches
  Living Room Grand – 5 ft 10 inches
  Professional Grand – 6 ft
  Drawing Room Grand – 6 ft 4 inches
  Parlour Grand – 6 ft 8 inches
  Half Concert Grand – 7 ft 4 inches
  Concert Grand – 8 ft 11 inches or longer

- The Seven Children of Baron von Trapp of
  The Sound of Music fame
  Liesel
  Friedrich
  Louisa
  Brigitta
  Kurt
  Marta
  Gretl

- The Seven Colours of the Rainbow
  Red
  Orange
  Yellow
  Green
  Blue
  Indigo
  Violet

SEVENS

- The Seven Days of Creation
  Created heaven and earth; day and night.
  Divided heaven from earth.
  Created the land, the sea and vegetation.
  Created the sun, the moon and the stars.
  Created creatures great and small.
  Created mankind.
  Sanctified the seventh day as the day of rest.

- The Seven Hills of Rome
  Palatine
  Capitoline
  Quirinal
  Viminal
  Esquiline
  Caelian
  Aventine

- The Seven Ages of Man (according to Shakespeare)
  The Infant
  The Schoolboy
  The Lover
  The Soldier
  The Justice
  The Pantaloon
  The Second Childhood

SEVENS

- The Seven Japanese Gods of Luck
  Bishamon
  Daikoku
  Ebisu
  Fukurokuju
  Jurojin
  Hotei
  Benten

- From 1940 to 1962, Bing Crosby and Bob Hope made seven road movies. The seven destinations were:
  Rio
  Hong Kong
  Singapore
  Zanzibar
  Morocco
  Utopia
  Bali

- The Seven Ionian Islands
  Corfu
  Cephalonia
  Zacynthus
  Leucas
  Ithaca
  Cythera
  Paxos

SEVENS

- The Seven Medieval Champions of Christendom
  St George – England
  St Denis – France
  St James – Spain
  St Anthony – Italy
  St Andrew – Scotland
  St Patrick – Ireland
  St David – Wales

- The Seven Gifts of the Holy Spirit
  Wisdom
  Understanding
  Counsel
  Fortitude
  Knowledge
  Piety
  Fear of the Lord

- The Seven Sisters

- The seven stars in the Taurus constellation visible to the naked eye, named after the daughters of the Titan Atlas and the Oceanid Pleione in Greek mythology:
  Alcyone
  Maia
  Electra

SEVENS

Merope
Taygete
Celaeno
Asterope

- The Seven Spiritual Works of Mercy
  To convert the sinner.
  To instruct the ignorant.
  To counsel those in doubt.
  To comfort those in doubt.
  To bear wrongs patiently.
  To forgive injuries.
  To pray for the living and the dead.

- The Seven Corporal Works of Mercy
  To tend the sick.
  To feed the hungry.
  To give drink to the thirsty.
  To clothe the naked.
  To harbour the stranger.
  To minister to prisoners.
  To bury the dead.

8

USELESS MIX

USELESS MIX

- America's Internal Revenue Service employees' tax manual has instructions for collecting taxes after a nuclear war.

- The only wood ever used by renowned English cabinet-maker Thomas Chippendale was mahogany.

- The typing exercise 'Now is the time for all good men to come to the aid of the party' was created by Charles E Weller.

- A year is exactly 365 days 5 hours 48 minutes and 46 seconds long.

- Khaki was first adopted for military uniforms in 1880 in the Afghan war. Only then was it finally admitted it was the best camouflage colour.

- In an amazing demonstration, crack shot Annie Oakley, using an ordinary rifle, once shot at 5,000 pennies, tossed into the air one after the other, and hit an incredible 4,777, giving her a 96% success rate.

- A bear was the first creature to test an ejection seat from a supersonic aircraft in 1962. It was ejected at 35,000 ft (10,668 m) and made a safe descent by parachute.

-------------------- USELESS MIX --------------------

- The average lifespan of a Stone Age caveman was eighteen years.

- *Playboar Magazine* has a centrefold that features the littermate of the month.

- In 1970 the Procrastinators' Club of America demanded a full refund for the Liberty Bell from London's Whitechapel Foundry because it had cracked in 1835. The foundry graciously agreed – provided the defective item could be returned in its original packaging.

- The words 'atomic bomb' were coined by H G Wells in his science-fiction story *The World Set Free*, written in 1914.

- The rocket launch countdown from ten to one stemmed from a 1928 German silent movie, *The Girl in the Moon*, in which director Fritz Lang reversed the count to build suspense.

- More diamonds are bought for Christmas (31%) than for any other event of the year.

- The average suit of armour for a medieval knight weighed between 50 and 55 lb (23–25 kg).

---------------------------- **USELESS MIX** ----------------------------

- The highest wind speed every recorded on earth was in New Hampshire, in the United States, on 24 April 1934. It was 231 mph (372 kph).

- If all the water was removed from the body of an average 160 lb (73 kg) man there would be just 64 lb (29 kg) of corpse left.

- The amethyst was once considered a charm against becoming drunk. The Greek word '*amethystos*', from which it is derived, means 'remedy for drunkenness'.

- A Boeing 747 airliner holds 57,285 gallons (260,418 litres) of fuel.

- Until 153BC New Year's Day fell in March. The Romans then switched to starting the New Year on 1 January.

- Supermodel Cindy Crawford was valedictorian of her high-school class and won a full college scholarship to study chemical engineering at Northwestern University in Evanston, Illinios. She dropped out after one term to take up a career in modelling.

- The Greek philosopher Socrates was trained as a stone cutter.

USELESS MIX

- Adolf Hitler's sister-in-law worked in New York City for the British War Relief during World War II. Bridget Hitler was the Irish-born wife of Hitler's older half-brother, Alois.

- Hugh Hefner's all-black private jet was named Big Bunny.

- In his New Year's Day column US journalist Westbrook Pegler repeated the same sentence 50 times. It was: 'I will never mix gin, beer and whiskey again.'

- 'Silent Night' was first played on a harp.

- Chilean Nylons and Australian Bananas are both types of shrimp.

- When Winston Churchill learned that Hitler had dubbed his country home Eagle's Nest he called his English country home Chartwell 'Cosy Pig'.

- The life expectancy of a modern toilet is 50 years.

- The first man to use the phrase 'The bigger they are the harder they fall' was heavyweight boxer Bob Fitzsimmons. He was talking of champion James J Jeffries, whom he fought in 1902. Fitzsimmons lost.

———————————— **USELESS MIX** ————————————

- British seaman James Bartley was swallowed alive by a whale in 1891 and survived for two days in its stomach before being released by his shipmates. He lived another 35 years to tell the tale.

- Dutch children put out shoes instead of stockings to receive their Christmas presents.

- The first *Playboy* centrefold in 1953 was Marilyn Monroe.

- The idea of flying a flag at half-mast as a sign of mourning came from the navy, where the top of the mast would be left empty for the invisible flag of death during a funeral at sea in the seventeenth century. The standard flag would be lowered to leave the mast top empty.

- Film star Hedy Lamarr was co-inventor of a system to radar control torpedoes at moving ships.

- The Nobel Peace Prize medal depicts three naked men with their hands on each other's shoulders.

- When Robert Louis Stevenson died in December 1894 he left his 13 November birthday to a friend in his will. She had always hated having a Christmas birthday.

USELESS MIX

- A poem written to celebrate a wedding is called an epithalamium.

- Buckingham Palace in London has more than 600 rooms.

- There are 412 doors in the White House.

- The first country to impose a general income tax was Britain, in 1799. It was done as a temporary measure to finance the war against Napoleon.

- The ancient Peruvian Inca Indians took off their sandals and handed them to each other to cement their marriage vows. It was the only formal moment in the ceremony.

- Actor Paul Newman was disqualified from the navy's pilot training programme during World War II because he is colour blind.

- The letters KGB stand for *Komitet gosudarstvennoi bezopasnosti* ('Committee of State Security').

- Coca-Cola was originally green.

- Clocks made before 1687 only had an hour hand.

--------------------- **USELESS MIX** ---------------------

- Tomb robbers were convinced that knocking the noses off Egyptian sarcophagi would prevent curses having effect.

- The average grave is 7 ft 8 inches (2 m 20 cm) by 3 ft 2 inches (0.9 m 5 cm) by 6 ft (2 m).

- A syzygy occurs when all the planets in the solar system align.

- The making of bottle caps in the United States uses more steel production than is used in building motor-car bodies.

- Approximately 25,200 umbrellas are lost each year on the British transport system.

- The Boston University bridge is the only place in the world where a boat can sail under a train driving under a car driving under an aeroplane.

- When a waitress in America draws a happy face on a meal bill her tips go up by 18%. If a waiter does the same, his tips rise by only 3% on average.

- On a Sunday in Salt Lake City, Utah, you can be fined up to £1,000 (about $1,600) for whistling.

USELESS MIX

- When Hitler announced the founding of the Third Reich he declared the first two to have been the Holy Roman Empire of Charlemagne and the second the German Empire founded by Bismarck in 1871.

- The Lincoln Memorial has 36 Doric columns. These represent the number of states in the union at the time of his death.

- The average soldier in World War I was three-quarters of an inch (2 cm) shorter than the average soldier in World War II.

- The first ever world summit on 'toilets' was held in Singapore in November 2001.

- The average typist uses the left hand 56% of the time.

- The brain of Neanderthal man was bigger than that of modern man.

- The Hoochinoo Indians provided the nickname 'Hooch' for alcohol. They produced an incredibly strong liquor that knocked people senseless.

- The international dialling code for Antarctica is 672.

USELESS MIX

- The watermelon-seed-spitting world record is 65 ft 4 inches (20 m 10 cm).

- A pin-up photo of film star Rita Hayworth was stuck to the first atomic bomb to be tested on the Bikini atoll, in the western Pacific, in 1946.

- The quadrature of a circle is a square with an area equal to that of the circle.

- The only inanimate symbol in the zodiac is Libra – the scales.

- By the time they are twenty years of age the average Western person has been exposed to over one million television commercials.

- The only state in America that has never recorded a temperature lower than 0 °F (-18 °C) is Hawaii.

- Ninety-six per cent of all women think that all toilets should be cleaned once a week.

- The abbreviation AD (Anno Domini), the year of our Lord, should properly be placed in front of the year – thus 500 BC but AD 2003.

─────────────── **USELESS MIX** ───────────────

- The Philip Morris Tobacco Company's crest bears Ceasar's Latin words '*Veni, vidi vici*' – 'I came, I saw I conquered'.

- At the battle of Waterloo Napoleon's white horse was called Marengo and Wellington rode the chestnut Copenhagen. They were named after the two men's famous victories.

- One in every six guns in the world is an AK-47.

- The longest flight every recorded of a propane explosion was when a railroad tanker car was thrown 3,000 ft (914 m) after it exploded during a train crash in Illinois, US. It also demolished a steel tower in its path.

- British royalty is rather slow to catch up with the modern world. Foreign ambassadors are still described as 'Ambassadors to the Court of St James', which was the royal palace before Buckingham Palace was built.

- To fall over, a bowling pin need only tilt 7.5°.

- A cyclic number is one where the digits all appear in the same order but rotate around when multiplied by any number from one to six. For example: 142,857 x 2 = 285,714; 142,857 x 4 = 571,428; 142,857 x 6 = 857,142.

——————— USELESS MIX ———————

- The 'v' (versus) in the name of a court case does not stand for versus but for 'and' in civil proceedings or 'against' in criminal proceedings.

- 14 February was declared St Valentine's Day in AD 498 by Pope Gelasius.

- Oak trees do not bear acorns until they are at least 50 years old.

- Japanese golfers are advised to take out hole-in-one insurance. Traditionally, in Japan a golfer sends gifts to their friends if they get a hole-in-one. It can often cost £10,000.

- Tribes that ages ago wanted to rid themselves of unwanted members without killing them used to burn their houses down so they would be forced to leave. Hence the expression 'to get fired'.

- The volume of the moon is the same volume as that of the Pacific Ocean.

- Clark Gable's army discharge papers were signed by Colonel Rudolf Abel in 1944. Abel was unmasked as a major Soviet spy in 1957.

--------------------- **USELESS MIX** ---------------------

- More beer than water was taken aboard the *Mayflower* before the Pilgrim Fathers set off on their epic journey from England.

- Hara-kiri is an impolite way of saying the Japanese word '*seppuku*' which literally means 'belly-splitting'.

- Mantles of gas lanterns are radioactive and will set off an alarm at a nuclear reactor.

- The only five-digit number to have the same digits in the reverse order when multiplied by four is 21,978. It comes to 87,912.

- The *Apollo 11* space vehicle had only 20 seconds of fuel left when it landed.

- Mexico once had three presidents in one day.

- People who are more educated are more likely to drink alcohol.

- In Moscow the skating rinks cover more than 250,000 sq. m of land during the winter.

- Presbyterians is an anagram of Britney Spears.

USELESS MIX

- Twenty-one per cent of American smokers do not believe that nicotine is addictive.

- In the London telephone directory the House of Lords comes between the House of Leather and the House of Love.

- Packard was the first motor-car company to replace the steering tiller with the steering wheel in 1900.

- The average motorist spends six months of their life waiting for traffic lights to change from red to green.

- Hallmark manufactures 105 different categories of greeting card.

- It was a dentist who invented the electric chair.

- The average driver will swear or blaspheme more than 32,000 times behind the wheel of their car in a lifetime.

- Seventy per cent of Americans who go to college say they do so just to make more money.

- M&Ms are said to have been developed so that soldiers could eat sweets without getting their fingers sticky.

—————————— **USELESS MIX** ——————————

● George Washington, a four-star general in his lifetime, was posthumously promoted to six-star general of the armies of congress by US President Jimmy Carter, who said America's first president should also be the highest-ranking military official.

● A seventeenth-century Swedish paleontologist claimed that in the Garden of Eden God spoke Swedish, Adam spoke Danish and the Serpent spoke French.

● According to the Holy Days and Fasting Days Act of 1551 every British citizen must attend a Christian church service on Christmas Day and must not use any kind of vehicle to get to the service. The law has never been repealed.

● Women recruits have to do a minimum of seventeen press-ups to pass the United States Army's basic training programme. Men must do 40.

● Rubber bands last longer if refrigerated.

● The average parent typically spends only nine minutes playing with their children on Christmas morning.

● A quarter of the bones in your body are in your feet.

—————————— USELESS MIX ——————————

- Degringolade means to fall and disintegrate.

- Japanese women always wear socks called '*tabi*' when wearing a kimono. The big toe of the sock is separated from the rest of the toes.

- Shang Sung turned a single piece of dough into 8,192 noodles in under a minute in Singapore on 31 July 1994.

- The Great Fire of London in 1666 destroyed half the city but injured only six people.

- In Guatemala Christmas Day is celebrated on 31 October.

- Worcestershire sauce is basically an anchovy ketchup.

- An average human produces enough saliva in a lifetime to fill two standard-sized swimming pools.

- The sun's rays that shine down through the clouds are called crepuscular rays.

- Coconuts kill more people in the world each year than sharks do. Sharks kill about 150 and coconuts kill some 2,000.

—————————— **USELESS MIX** ——————————

- The growth rate of some bamboo plants reaches up to 3 ft (0.9 m) per day.

- We blink about 84 million times a year.

- It is an offence in Britain, with up to a five-year jail sentence, to riotously demolish a hovel.

- The Aztec emperor Montezuma had a nephew, Cuitlahuac, whose name meant 'plenty of excrement'.

- Lemons have more sugar than oranges.

- The Empire State Building in New York has 1,575 steps from the ground floor to the top.

- The asteroid that is believed to have caused the death of the dinosaurs was named Chicxulub.

- Charlie Brown would be four and a half feet (about one metre) tall if he were a real person. His head would take up 2 ft (0.6 m) of this.

- General George Custer, the hero of the Battle of Little Bighorn, graduated bottom of his West Point class in 1861.

USELESS MIX

- The naval rank of admiral is derived from the Arabic phrase *'amīr-al-bahr*, which means 'lord of the sea'.

- Currently there are estimated to be more $100 bills in Russia than there are in the United States.

- A full moon is nine times brighter than a half moon.

- The bread slots in a toaster are called toast wells.

- SOS was chosen as the Morse emergency code in 1908 because the letters 'S' and 'O' are the easiest to remember and key in. 'S' equals dot dot dot; 'O' equals dash dash dash. It does not stand for Save Our Souls.

- The most popular car colour in the world is red.

- Pound for pound, hamburgers cost more then new cars.

- The average acre of corn contains 7.2 million kernels.

- The cigarette lighter was invented before the match.

- The full, official, name of Jesus College, Cambridge, is 'The College of the Holy Trinity and the most Blessed and Exalted Virgin St Radegund'.

────────── USELESS MIX ──────────

- Only seven prisoners were liberated when the Bastille was stormed in 1789 at the start of the French Revolution.

- Shakespeare is believed to have been 46 when the King James version of the Bible was written. In psalm 46 the 46th word from the first word is 'shake' and the 46th word from the last word is 'spear'.

- There are nearly half a million sauna baths in Finland.

- The three most valuable brand names on earth are Marlboro, Coca-Cola and Budweiser, in that order.
- The revolving door was invented in 1888.

- Thirty-five per cent of the people who use personal ads for dating are already married.

- The top layer of a wedding cake is known as the Groom's Cake and is usually made of fruit. It easily survives until the first anniversary when the couple eat it.

- The San Francisco cable cars are the only mobile national monuments in America.

- Months that begin on a Sunday always contain a Friday the thirteenth.

─────────── **USELESS MIX** ───────────

● The average person falls asleep in seven minutes.

● When the atomic bomb exploded on Hiroshima, 61,825 homes were destroyed.

● Marlboro's first owner died of lung cancer.

● The snapping turtle, which eats carrion, is used by police in some countries to find dead bodies in lakes, ponds and swamps.

● The King of Hearts is the only king without a moustache in a playing-card deck.

● There are more reverse-charge telephone calls on Father's Day than on any other day of the year.

● A gold razor removed from King Tutankhamen's tomb was still sharp enough to be used.

● The film star who achieved the highest military rank ever was James Stewart who became a brigadier general.

● Pavst beer won a Blue Ribbon at the Chicago Fair in 1893. And Milwaukee's Pavst Beer is still sold – over a hundred years later – as Pavst Blue Ribbon Beer.

──────────── **USELESS MIX** ────────────

- At its most powerful in 400 BC the Greek City of Sparta had 25,000 citizens – but 50,000 slaves.

- Napoleon Bonaparte's mother's name was Laticia.

- The 'you are here' arrow on maps is called the 'ideo locator'.

- The penultimate is the one before the last. The one before that is the antipenultimate.

- The glue on Israeli postage stamps is kosher.

- The United States sued Great Britain for damages caused by them building ships for the confederacy during the American Civil War. They initially asked for $1 billion – but settled on £25 million.

- Fifteen per cent of women in the United States send themselves flowers on Valentine's Day.

- Police issue tickets for driving too slow on Germany's Autobahn.

- Until 1857 Spanish doubloons were still legal tender in the United States.

USELESS MIX

- Tights became the best-selling leg covering for women after Mary Quant created the mini skirt in the 60s. The mini skirt demanded a leg covering that went all the way up to the bottom.

- There is a spoon museum in New Jersey, US, which has over 5,400 spoons from every state, and almost every country, in the world.

- The British flag is properly known as the Union Flag. It is called the Union Jack only when flown on board a naval ship.

- American Indian code-makers in World War II used the Comanche phrase *posah-tai-do* as their name for Hitler. It means 'Crazy White Man'.

- The external tank on the space shuttle is not painted.

- In American military terminology a shovel is known as a 'combat emplacement evacuator'.

- It is illegal to frown at cows in Bladworth, Saskatchewan.

- Forty per cent of American adults expect to gain weight during the Christmas holiday season.

USELESS MIX

- Man and monkeys are the only mammals that can distinguish colours.

- More first babies are born in the sixth month after marriage than at any other time.

- If the whole population of China jumped up and down at the same time, the vibration could create a tidal wave that would engulf the United States.

- The granite removed to make way for the foundations of each new building in New York weighs more than the actual building, resulting in Manhattan getting lighter each year.

- The Daimler Conquest was named after its then price of £1,066.

- 'Jingle Bells' was originally written for Thanksgiving.

- A Malagasy Indian male cannot shave by tribal law until after his father is dead.

- A seven-year-old elephant was awarded £1,750 damages by California Supreme Court Judge Turtle when it lost its ability to water-ski after a motor accident.

USELESS MIX

- Organised crime in the United States represents one tenth of the national income.

- A sabre-toothed cat called a smilodon lived during the Pleistocene age.

- Both General George Custer and Chief Crazy Horse of the Sioux Indians, protaganists at the Battle of the Little Bighorn, were called 'curly' as children.

- The first Christmas card is said to have been sent in 1843 from artist John Horsley to his friend Sir Henry Cole.

- The smile is the only physical gesture that man does not share with other animals.

- Out of 2,250,000 pianos in Britain 1,800,000 of them are said to be out of tune at any given moment.

- There is a special squad of police in Amsterdam whose only duty is to cope with motorists who drive their vehicles into the city's canals.

- Blackbeard the pirate would tuck slow-burning fuses under his tricorne hat – wreathing his head in black smoke – to frighten his opponents in battle.

—————— USELESS MIX——————

- It is against the law to be a prostitute in Siena, Italy, if your name is Mary.

- It takes 22 hours to make Smarties from scratch and we eat 16,000 a minute in the United Kingdom.

- There are an estimated 400,000 camels in Australia, descendants of the pack animals taken there in the nineteenth century, and some are exported to Saudi Arabia to provide food in restaurants.

- In the sixteenth century the law in England allowed men to beat their wives – but only before 10 pm.

- 'Freelance' comes from the knights whose lances were free for hire and who were not pledged to one master.

- Medieval knights put shark's skin on their sword handles to give them a more secure grip. They would dig the shark's scales into their palms.

- The flagpole at the Tokyo Olympics was 48ft 10 ¾ inches (15 m 27 cm) tall.

- Eighty-five per cent of people can curl their tongues into a tube.

―――――――――――― **USELESS MIX** ――――――――――――

● On an average day Canada imports some 822 Russian-made hockey sticks.

● In medieval castles spiral staircases ran clockwise. Soldiers were always trained to fight right-handed, so when an invading force reached the staircase their sword-wielding hands would not be able to reach around the central column of the stairs. This left them vulnerable to the defending forces as they climbed up.

● The Duke of Wellington was an expert yo-yo player. The game was then known as a 'bandalore'.

● The term for one sixty-fourth of a musical note is a hemidemisemiquaver.

● Technically the banana is a berry.

● Edward Drinker Cope, an American paleontologist of the late nineteenth century, provided the skull for the type specimen for the human species. A type specimen is used in paleontology as the best example of that species.

● The scent on the artificial rabbit used in greyhound racing is anise.

──────────── **USELESS MIX** ────────────

- In a recent year, of the 317 shootings by New York City police officers 27% of the victims were dogs.

- Croatia was the first country to recognise the United States in 1776.

- When the German spy Mata Hari went before the firing squad in October 1917, she dressed all in black – including black silk stockings, kid gloves and a large floppy black hat with a black silk ribbon.

- Alabama was the first US state to legalise the celebration of Christmas. The last state to make Christmas a legal holiday was Oklahoma in 1907.

- An earthquake on 16 December 1811 forced the Mississippi River to flow backwards.

- There is a one-in-seven chance of a burglary being solved in the United States.

- A full-grown pumpkin vine has an average fifteen miles (24 km) of roots.

- Americans consume 5,200,000 lb (2,358,720 kg) of pickles each day.

─────────── USELESS MIX ───────────

- When George Washington was elected president there was a king in France, a czarina in Russia, an emperor in China and a shogun in Japan. Of these, only the presidency remains.

- America's first nudist organisation was founded in 1929 by three men.

- In Syria Christmas gifts are delivered not by Santa Claus but by one of the wise men's camels.

- There are over 13,000 knives, forks and spoons in the White House.

- If in a statue a person is mounted on a horse, and the horse has both its front legs in the air, the person died in battle. If one leg is in the air, the person died as a result of wounds received in battle. If the person died of natural causes then all four of the horse's legs are on the ground.

- Any number when squared is equal to just one more than the multiplication of the two numbers on either side of it. For example: 5 x 5 = 25 and 4 x 6 = 24 – a difference of one. Or: 7 x 7 = 49 and 6 x 8 = 48 – again a difference of one.

USELESS MIX

- The Spanish equivalent of UFO is OVNI, which stands for *Objeto Volador No Identificado*.

- Americans dispose of 1.6 billion pens a year.

- It took Napoleon only four hours to send a message from Rome to Paris – almost 700 miles (1,127 km) – using a semaphore system from hilltop to hilltop.

- The saguaro cactus, which is found in south-western United States, does not grow branches until it is between 60 and 75 years old.

- Non-smokers dream more than smokers do.

- Grapes explode when heated in a microwave oven.

- Crack received its name because it crackles when you smoke it.

- In the four years from 1347 to 1351 the Black Death plague reduced the population of Europe by a third.

- The only part of the United Kingdom occupied by Nazis during World War II was Jersey in the Channel Isles.

USELESS MIX

- A zarf is the holder of a handleless coffee cup.

- All Confederate army officers were given copies of Victor Hugo's *Les Misérables*. Robert E Lee believed the book symbolised their cause. Both revolts were defeated.

- The opening bars of Beethoven's *Fifth Symphony* preceded all BBC radio broadcasts to Europe during World War II because it sounded like the Morse code for the letter 'v' for victory.

- Revolvers cannot be fitted with silencers. The gases escape the cylinder gaps at the rear of the barrel and cannot be prevented from making a noise by a device fitted to the end of the barrel.

- The 'crack' of a whip is actually a miniature sonic boom as the tip of the whip breaks the sound barrier.

- In Norway they hide all the household brooms on Christmas Eve. It was once believed that witches came out on Christmas Eve and stole the brooms to ride the skies.

- Astronauts cannot cry in space because there is no gravity to assist the tear flow.

——————— USELESS MIX ———————

- The Eiffel Tower in Paris has 1,792 steps.

- St Stephen is the patron saint of bricklayers.

- The average smell weighs about 760 nanograms.

- Napoleon Bonaparte's official emblem was the bumblebee.

- In the British version of the board game Monopoly the most expensive property, Mayfair, is not a street but a district in the West End of London.

- The buzz generated by an electric razor in America is in the key of B flat.

- In the Ukraine a spider's web found on Christmas morning is supposed to bring good luck. For this reason an artificial spider and web is often the main tree decoration in Ukrainian homes.

- Armoured knights would raise their visors to identify themselves when they rode past the king. This habit is the origin of the modern military salute.

- The Americans tried to train bats to drop bombs during World War II.

─────────── **USELESS MIX** ───────────

- The world's biggest bell is the Tsar Karokal, which weighs 216 tons (219,467 kg) and was cast in the Kremlin in 1733. It is cracked and cannot be rung.

- The Führer of Germany at the end of World War II was Grand Admiral Karl Doenitz. He took over after Hitler's suicide, a week before the Nazi surrender in 1945.

- The Pentagon in Washington DC has five sides, five stories and five acres in the middle.

- A pack-a-day smoker will, on average, lose two teeth every ten years.

- The first product to have a bar code was Wrigley's chewing gum.

- Hydrangeas tend to produce pink and white flowers in alkaline soil and blue flowers in acidic soil.

- The world's oldest whiskey distillery is in Ireland and was founded in 1657.

- In Caracas, Venezuela, it is now customary to roller skate to church on Christmas Eve and the streets are blocked off so this unusual tradition can be catered for.

————————— USELESS MIX —————————

- Benjamin Davis became the first ever black general in history in the US Army, in 1940. His son, Benjamin Davis Jr, became the first black general in history in the US Air Force, in 1954.

- Women started removing hair from their legs in 400 BC. They either plucked them with tweezers or singed them with a flame.

- To 'testify' was based on men in the Roman court guaranteeing a statement by swearing on their testicles.

- There are more chickens in the world than there are people.

- The first underground school to be built was the Abo Elementary School in Artesia, New Mexico, in 1976.

- A hurricane releases more energy in ten minutes than all the nuclear weapons combined.

- There are eight sizes of Champagne container, starting with a bottle and ending with the largest, which is called a Nebuchadnezzar – after the biblical king.

- Scotland exports sand to Saudi Arabia.

─────────── **USELESS MIX** ───────────

- The White House had its first Christmas tree in 1856. It was decorated by US President Franklyn Pierce.

- Moses, Charles Darwin, Aristotle and Sir Isaac Newton all had bad stutters.

- The highest-scoring word in the English language game of Scrabble is 'quartzy'. This scores 164 points if played across a red, triple-word square, with the 'z' on a light blue letter square. It would score 162 points if played across two pink double-word squares with the 'q' and the 'y' on those squares. 'Bezique' and 'cazique' are the next highest-scoring words, with a possible 161 points each.

- Sagittarius is the most southerly of the zodiac constellations.

- In his lifetime an average man will spend 3,350 hours shaving – or 139 ½ days.

- The names of the three wise monkeys are: Mizaru – see no evil; Mikazaru – hear no evil; and Mozaru – speak no evil.

- Until the late nineteenth century British sailors were forbidden to use forks as they were considered unmanly and harmful to discipline.

USELESS MIX

- If you cut a piece of paper in half, place the two pieces on top of each other and cut them in half again and again, until you have done it 60 times, the stack of paper will reach to the sun and back.

- The total of the consecutive numbers from one to 100 when added is 5,050.

- The world record for non-stop rocking in a rocking chair is 440 hours.

- There have been more than 250,000 Elvis sightings since his death.

- The soma plant is thought to be sacred in India where over a hundred hymns are dedicated to it.

- Contrary to popular folklore, cuckoo clocks do not come from Switzerland but from the Black Forest in Germany.

- The man who replaced Manfred von Richthofen, as leader of the 'Flying Circus' fighter squadron in World War I after he was killed was Hermann Goering – who went on to become head of the German Luftwaffe.

USELESS MIX

- More than 50% of the video-games market is adult.

- Seventy per cent of household dust is dead skin cells.

- The patron saint of Oxford is Saint Frideswide, and female children in Oxford are sometimes christened Friday after her nickname.

- England's three largest landowners are the Queen, the Church of England and Trinity College Cambridge.

- The first atomic bomb dropped on Japan was released from *Enola Gay*, which was named after the unit commander's mother. The second bomb was dropped from *Bock's Car*.

- The top three cork-producing countries are Spain, Portugal and Algeria.

- Originally there was a thirteenth zodiac constellation – Ophercus. But astrologers ignored it because of thirteen being an unlucky number.

- The internal combustion engine motor car was first produced in 1886. Ten years later the first recorded car theft occurred.

USELESS MIX

- Raindrops are not teardrop-shaped; they are rounded at the top and flat on the bottom.

- Socks – first found in Egyptian tombs – remained popular for 5,000 years, until the fifteenth century and the introduction of tights.

- The tablet carried by the Statue of Liberty is 2 ft (0.6 m) thick.

- The toothbrush was invented in 1498.

- The asking price for a small piece of coal recovered from the wreckage of the *Titanic* is £17.50.

- According to ceremonial custom among orthodox Jews, it is officially sundown when you cannot tell the difference between a black thread and a red one.

- Useless Facts and Trivia Day is on 9 March.

- The liner *Queen Elizabeth the Second* should always be written *QE2* because QEII is the Queen herself.

- Every month has its ides – not just March, when Julius Ceasar was killed.

USELESS MIX

- The Egyptian hieroglyph for the figure 100,000 is a tadpole.

- Pantalettes were designed in Victorian times to conceal limb areas not covered by skirts. Victorians even used them to cover table legs.

- Groaking is to watch people eating food in the hope that they will offer you some.

- Trousers for women only became acceptable wear in the 1930s during the Great Depression.

- Houdini actually trained his pet dog to escape from a miniature set of handcuffs.

- Dynamite contains monkey nuts as an ingredient.

GEOGRAPHY, SPACE FACTS AND TRAVEL

— GEOGRAPHY, SPACE FACTS AND TRAVEL —

- Rock English, a mixture of Spanish and English, is the local language spoken in Gibraltar.

- The English gold coin, the guinea, is named after the country in West Africa where the gold used to make it was originally mined.

- The Red Sea is so named after the algae that when dying turns the Red Sea's normally intense blue-green waters to red.

- In Verona, Italy, in which Shakespeare set his tragedy *Romeo and Juliet*, about a thousand letters arrive addressed to Juliet every Valentine's Day.

- The official name for Switzerland is the French 'Confédération Helvétique' – or the Helvetic Confederation. These initials provide the CH international symbol for Switzerland, which make up car registration plates, stickers and e-mail addresses.

- In Iceland Domino's Pizza has reindeer sausage pie on its menu.

- A large number of boulders that have fallen off a cliff is known as 'talus'.

—GEOGRAPHY, SPACE FACTS AND TRAVEL—

- In New Guinea more than 700 different native languages are spoken — which is a third of the world's known languages.

- The highest point in Pennsylvania is lower than the lowest point in Colorado.

- The first European to see New Zealand was Abel Tasman in 1642, but the first to set foot on the island was James Cook in 1769.

- Lake Nicaragua in Nicaragua has the only freshwater sharks in the world.

- If the ozone in the atmosphere were compressed to a pressure equal to that at the earth's surface, the layer would be only 3 mm thick.

- There is a town named Santa Claus in Indiana, USA.

- Ethiopia means 'the land of sunburned faces' in Greek.

- The political divisions of Japan are called 'prefectures', whereas those of Switzerland are called 'cantons'.

- Twenty-eight per cent of Africa is wilderness.

— GEOGRAPHY, SPACE FACTS AND TRAVEL —

- Thirty-eight per cent of North America is wilderness.

- Venus is the only planet that rotates clockwise.

- The only place in the world where alligators and crocodiles coexist is in Florida.

- Two thousand pounds (907 kg) of space dust and other debris falls on the earth every day.

- A *daibutsu* is a giant Buddha in Japan.

- In Italy it is illegal to make coffins out of anything except nutshells or wood.

- New Zealand was named after Abel Tasman's home district, Zealand, in the Netherlands.

- The moon weighs 81,000 trillion tons.

- The six official languages of the United Nations are English, French, Arabic, Chinese, Russian and Spanish.

- The only river to flow both north and south of the equator is the Congo River, which crosses the equator twice.

—GEOGRAPHY, SPACE FACTS AND TRAVEL—

- Three hundred years ago most Egyptians died before they were 30.

- The Sitka spruce is Britain's most commonly planted tree.

- Nullarbor Plain in south-west Australia gets its name from the Latin *nullus arbor* – 'no tree'.

- Earth was named after Terra, the Roman god of the land.

- Ninety-nine per cent of the buildings in Reykjavik, the capital of Iceland, are heated by natural hot springs.

- The Bridge of Sighs in Venice received its centuries-old name after the sighs of prisoners being taken across the bridge from the judgement hall in the doge's palace on one side to the dungeons and execution cell in the state prison on the other.

- The Bronx in New York City is named after the Bronx River. The Bronx River is named after the first European settler in the Bronx – the Scandanavian-born Jonas Bronck, who settled there in 1639.

- The tiniest port in Canada is Port Williams, Nova Scotia.

—GEOGRAPHY, SPACE FACTS AND TRAVEL —

- If you told someone they were 'one in a million' you would be saying it to about two thousand of them in China.

- The national flower of Greenland is the willow herb.

- Monaco has the biggest per-capita ownership of Rolls Royce cars in the world. In the last survey, in the early 1990s, the figure was one for every 65.1 people.

- Desire Street, in New Orleans, runs directly alongside and parallel with Piety Street.

- Hawaii has only two snakes: a sea snake that is rarely seen and a blind snake that lives like an earthworm.

- Zaire is the world leader in cobalt mining, producing two-thirds of the world's cobalt supply.

- The London Underground station St John's Wood is the only station on the network that does not contain any of the letters of the word 'mackerel'.

- On the Pacific Gilbert and Ellis Islands, Britain's largest colonial territory, the highest point above sea level is 11 ft (3 m).

—GEOGRAPHY, SPACE FACTS AND TRAVEL—

- The roads on the island of Guam are made of coral. This is because the ground coral sand of the beaches is used to mix concrete instead of importing regular sand from thousands of miles away.

- The national anthem of the Netherlands is the oldest national anthem in the world. The music appeared in 1572 and the lyrics in 1590.

- The oldest surviving parliament is in Iceland. It first met in 930 when Viking chieftains met in the open air to argue their differences.

- The floral emblem of Western Australia is the Mangles' kangaroo paw.

- Mount Cook in New Zealand is the largest mountain in Oceana, at 3,764 m.

- The driest place on earth is a series of valleys near Ross Island in Antarctica, where for at least the last two million years no rain has ever fallen.

- Only five nations in Europe touch just one other: Portugal, Denmark, San Marino, Vatican City and Monaco.

—GEOGRAPHY, SPACE FACTS AND TRAVEL —

- Devon is the only county in Great Britain to have two coasts.

- The city of Mount Vernon, in Washington, US, claims to produce more tulip blooms annually than Holland.

- Swahili is a combination of Arabic, Portuguese and African tribal languages.

- Tiny clouds that seem to have broken away from bigger clouds are called scuds.

- There are now said to be more Samoans in Los Angeles than in American Samoa.

- About one-tenth of the world's surface is permanently covered in ice.

- The smallest and shallowest ocean in the world is the Arctic Ocean.

- The Hudson River, running alongside Manhattan, can run in either direction depending on the tide.

- The three best-known Western names in China are Jesus Christ, Richard Nixon and Elvis Presley.

—GEOGRAPHY, SPACE FACTS AND TRAVEL—

- Giraffe tails, woodpecker scalps and porpoise teeth have all been used as money, somewhere in the world.

- Three times the size of Everest, the largest volcano in our solar system is Olympus Mons on Mars.

- The Channel grows 300 mm each year.

- Cueta in Spain is actually located in Africa, just across the Straits of Gibraltar.

- A Saudi Arabian woman can get a divorce if her husband does not give her coffee.

- The capital of Eritrea is Asmara.

- Woodward Avenue in Detroit, Michigan, carries the designation M-1 because it was the first paved road anywhere in the world.

- To eat in the Eiffel Tour restaurant you now have to go to New Orleans in Louisiana, where the dismantled restaurant from the famous Paris landmark was reassembled and reopened for business in 1986.

- Tasmania has the cleanest air in the inhabited world.

— GEOGRAPHY, SPACE FACTS AND TRAVEL —

- The word for 'name' in Japanese is '*na-ma-e*'. In Mongolian it is '*nameg*'.

- There is a Historical Museum of Spaghetti in Pontedassio, Italy.

- Seoul, the South Korean capital, means just 'capital' in the Korean language.

- The most important sites in Beijing were built by foreigners: the Forbidden City was built by the Mongols and the Temple of Heaven was built by the Manchurians.

- Jupiter is bigger than all the other planets in our solar system combined.

- The only reasonably sized town in the world whose name begins with ABC is the Dutch town of Abcoudi.

- The Niagara Falls have eaten their way seven miles (11 km) up stream since their formation 10,000 years ago. If erosion continues at this rate they will disappear into Lake Erie in 22,000 years.

- The Dominican Republic, Mexico, Zambia, Kiribati, Fiji and Egypt all have birds on their flags.

—GEOGRAPHY, SPACE FACTS AND TRAVEL—

- At latitude 60° south you can sail all the way around the world.

- South Africa used to have two official languages. Now it has eleven.

- The 1968 film *Krakatoa — East of Java* had a major fault. The volcano was in fact west of Java.

- Britain's shortest river is the Brun, which runs through Burnley in Lancashire.

- Toilets in Australia flush counter-clockwise.

- Hong Kong has the world's largest double-decker tram fleet.

- The highest wave ever recorded — towering a full ten-stories high — was 112 feet (34 m) high and seen in the North Pacific in 1933.

- The longest place name still in use belongs to a New Zealand hill — Taumatawhakatangihangakoauauotamateaturipukakapiki maungahoronukupokaiwhenuakitanatahu — with 85 letters.

— GEOGRAPHY, SPACE FACTS AND TRAVEL —

- The largest landlocked country in the world is Mongolia.

- Fifty-one countries joined the United Nations when it was founded in 1945. On its 50th birthday in 1995 it had 185 members.

- The oldest text for a national anthem is that of Japan, which dates to the ninth century. However, the music is from 1880.

- The average iceberg weighs 20 million tons.

- Oxford Street, in London, is named after the Earl of Oxford and not because it, coincidentally, is the start of the main road from London to Oxford.

- In its lifetime the earth has been hit by at least one million meteors.

- The town Spa, which gave its name to mineral springs everywhere, is located in Belgium.

- Brazoria county in south-east Texas is the only county in the United States to have every kind of poisonous snake found in the United States and Canada.

—GEOGRAPHY, SPACE FACTS AND TRAVEL—

- Louisiana's counties are actually called parishes – for example, Jefferson David Parish.

- Various types of lightning have been identified by meteorologists. The temperature of the Positive Giant type of lightning bolt reaches 30,000°C – over five times hotter than the surface of the sun.

- Canada is an Iroquoian Indian word meaning 'Big Village'.

- The earth's atmosphere is proportionately thinner than the skin of an apple.

- Lake Baikal, in southern Siberia, is the deepest lake in the world. It was formed 25 to 30 million years ago and is 1,743 m (5, 718 ft) deep.

- Ninety per cent of the world's ice is contained in the Antarctic ice sheet.

- Dildo is a town in Newfoundland, Canada.

- The red supergiant star Betelgeuse has a diameter larger than that of the earth's orbit around the sun – 186 million miles (299,329,800 km).

— GEOGRAPHY, SPACE FACTS AND TRAVEL —

- The oldest town in Belgium is Tongeren.

- Grand Rapids, Michigan, was the first city in the United States to put fluoride in its water supply.

- The longest highway in America is Route 6, which starts at Cape Cod in Massachusetts and goes through fourteen states before ending in Bishop, California.

- New Zealand is the only country that contains every type of climate in the world.

- Niagara Falls stopped flowing for 30 hours on 29 March 1848 because of an ice jam blocking the Niagara River.

- When members of the nature-worshipping Southern Indian tribe Todas greet one another they thumb their noses instead of shaking hands.

- The original cobble stones that were used to pave the streets in New York were originally weighting stones put in the hulls of ships to keep an even keel.

- Between 1947 and 1959 42 nuclear devices were detonated in the Marshall Islands, in the north-west Pacific.

—GEOGRAPHY, SPACE FACTS AND TRAVEL—

- Australian $5, $10, $20, $50 and $100 notes are made of plastic.

- There are only three types of snake on the island of Tasmania and they are all deadly poisonous.

- Alberta in Canada has been completely free of rats since 1905.

- If you stand with your eyes about 6 ft (2 m) above the surface of the ocean the horizon will be about 3 miles (5 km) away.

- The record for the most snowfall in one day was set on 7 May 1916 in Alaska when 78 inches (198 cm) fell.

- In 1929 Toronto, Ontario, in eastern Canada, became home to the biggest swimming pool in the world. The pool held 2,000 people and measured 300 by 75 ft (91 by 23 m). It is still in operation.

- The Netherlands and the United States both have national anthems that do not mention their countries' names.

- Lightning strikes about 6,000 times per minute on the earth.

— GEOGRAPHY, SPACE FACTS AND TRAVEL —

- When the University of Nebraska Cornhuskers play football at home the stadium becomes the third-largest city of the central US state.

- Singapore is the only country with only one train station.

- Cathedral Caverns near Grant, Alabama, US, has the world's largest cave opening, the world's largest stalagmite (Goliath) and the world's largest stalagmite forest.

- All the moons of the solar system are named according to Greek and Roman mythology, except the moons of Uranus, which are named after Shakespearean characters.

- Although Ohio is listed as the seventeenth state in the United States it is technically number 47. Until 7 August 1953 Congress forgot to vote on a resolution to admit Ohio to the Union.

- The world's biggest church all made of wood is Kerimski Church in Finland.

- The town of Tidikelt, in the Sahara desert, went ten years without rainfall.

—GEOGRAPHY, SPACE FACTS AND TRAVEL—

- Uranus's axis of rotation is inclined 98° to the plain of its orbit — which means that it rotates on its side.

- St Paul, Minnesota, was originally called Pig's Eye after a man who ran a saloon there.

- Vang is the most common surname among the Hmong people of Laos.

- The Angel of Independence in Mexico City was built by architect Antonio Rivas Mercado. The face of the angel is a portrait of his daughter.

- Quebec and Newfoundland are the only two Canadian provinces that do not allow personalised licence plates on cars.

- There are over 50,000 earthquakes a year around the world.

- If Brooklyn, New York, became independent of New York City it would become the third-largest city in the United States after the rest of New York and Los Angeles.

- Birmingham has more miles of canal than Venice.

— GEOGRAPHY, SPACE FACTS AND TRAVEL —

- Jamaica's main export is bauxite, which is used to make aluminium.

- In Venice, Italy, all gondolas must be painted black unless they belong to a senior official.

- Dublin is literally Ireland's Blackpool. In Irish its name comes from the words '*dubh linn*', which mean 'black pool'.

- Australia is the only continent without an active volcano.

- The inhabitants of Darwin, Australia, drink a yearly average of 62 gallons (282 litres) of beer each.

- Mexico's east coast is sinking into the sea at the rate of 1 or 2 cm a year.

- The country with the biggest percentage of female heads of household is Botswana.

- The German Bundestag, the Lower House of Parliament, is the world's largest elected legislative body, with 672 members.

- Cyprus has a map on its flag.

—GEOGRAPHY, SPACE FACTS AND TRAVEL—

- A hailstone containing a carp fell in Essen, Germany.

- Some Malaysians protect their babies from disease by bathing them in beer.

RELIGION AND
MYTHOLOGY

————RELIGION AND MYTHOLOGY————

- A bible published in England in 1632 missed out the word 'not' in the seventh commandment, making it 'Thou shalt commit adultery'. It became known as 'The Wicked Bible'.

- In February 1964 evangelist Billy Graham broke his life-long rule against watching television on Sunday – to see the Beatles' first appearance on American television.

- The latest day in the year on which Easter Sunday can fall is 25 April. The earliest is 22 March.

- The only woman whose age is mentioned in the Bible is Sarah, who bore Abraham a child, Isaac, when she was 90. She was said to die at the age of 127.

- The most common name in the Bible is Zechariah. There are 33 of them.

- At 6 cubits and a span, Goliath's height was somewhere between nine feet three inches (3 m 8 cm) and eleven feet nine inches (3 m 23 cm). A cubit is the distance from the elbow to the end of the middle finger and can vary from 17 to 22 inches (43 to 56 cm). A span is the distance from the extended little fingertip to the end of the thumb and is approximately nine inches (23 cm).

————RELIGION AND MYTHOLOGY————

- The Vikings had a god of snowshoes named Ull.

- There were three decks on Noah's ark.

- Methuselah lived to be 969 years old, according to Genesis.

- When W C Fields was caught glancing through a bible he explained it with the words: 'Looking for loopholes'.

- According to the Bible there are twelve pearly gates.

- In addition to the animals there were eight people on Noah's ark. Noah, his wife, his sons Shem, Ham and Japheth, and their wives.

- The three wise men were called Balthazar, Caspar and Melchior.

- Delilah had to cut seven tresses of hair from Samson's head to render him powerless.

- According to classical mythology the first mortal woman was Pandora.

- The goddess of the rainbow, in Greek mythology, was Iris.

RELIGION AND MYTHOLOGY

- Jesus is believed to have spoken Aramaic, the language then in use in the Arabian peninsular where he lived. A modern version of the language is still spoken in Syria.

- The New Testament was originally written in Greek.

- The world population at the time of the Crucifixion was about 200 million.

- Only one Englishman has become Pope in 2,000 years. He was Nicholas Breakspear, or Adrian IV, from 1154 to 1159.

- In New Mexico more than 11,000 people have visited a tortilla chip that has the face of Jesus Christ burned on it.

- On 29 November 2000 Pope John Paul II was made an honorary Harlem Globetrotter.

- Salome's dance was the only solo dance mentioned in the Bible.

- Xmas does not begin with the Roman letter X. It begins with the Greek letter '*chi*', which was used in medieval manuscripts as an abbreviation for the word 'Christ'. For example, 'Xus' equals 'Christus'.

──────RELIGION AND MYTHOLOGY──────

- The names of the two thieves crucified with Jesus were Dismas and Gestas.

- Some biblical scholars believe that Aramaic did not contain a way of saying 'many' and used a term that has come down to us as '40'. This means that when the Bible refers to 40 days it actually means 'many days'.

- Nell Gwynne once quietened an angry Oxford crowd, who mistakenly believed she was Charles II's French Catholic mistress, by telling them: 'Pray, good people, be civil. I am the Protestant whore.'

- Forty-three per cent of Americans regularly attend religious services.

- The city with the highest per-capita viewing of TV evangelists is Washington DC.

- The shortest verse in the Bible is 'Jesus wept'.

- The only domestic animal not mentioned in the Bible is the cat.

- Prince Charles once threw the moderator of the Church of Scotland into a fountain at Balmoral.

———RELIGION AND MYTHOLOGY———

- The American newspaper columnist H L Mencken wrote: 'Puritanism. The haunting fear that someone, somewhere, may be happy.'

- There are nine ranks of angels. From the highest to the lowest, they are Seraphims, Cherubims, Thrones, Dominions, Virtues, Powers, Principalities, Archangels and Angels.

- Moses was 120 years old when he died.

- The holy cities of Islam are Mecca, Medina and Jerusalem.

- There are 806 million Roman Catholics and 343 million Protestants.

- Buddha is known as 'The Enlightened One'.

- A church council in the twelfth century declared: 'A Christian man is bound to chastise his wife moderately.'

- Confucianism, founded by Confucius, has 175 million followers, mainly in China.

- Preachers who travelled on horseback through the old West were known as 'circuit riders'.

———RELIGION AND MYTHOLOGY———

- When Lady Carina Fitzalan Howard was asked if her future husband, television interviewer David Frost, was religious, she replied: 'Yes, he thinks he's God almighty.'

- The film *The Ten Commandments*, in which Charlton Heston plays Moses, was the biggest cinema box-office earner of the 1950s.

- Sonny and Cher, at the start of their careers, appeared in bible advertisements produced for the American Bible Society.

- The savage Salem witch trials in the seventeenth century were all based on a single line in Exodus: 'Thou shalt not suffer a witch to live.'

- The largest Catholic church in the United States is the Shrine of the Immaculate Conception in Washington DC.

- The first bible to be published in America was in the language of the Algonquian Indians.

- The Crystal Cathedral, founded by TV evangelist Robert Schuller, in Garden Grove, California, is longer than a football field and contains more than 10,000 panes of glass.

———— **RELIGION AND MYTHOLOGY** ————

- Lord Hugh Cecil believed 'the two dangers which beset the Church of England are good music and bad preaching'.

- Brigham Young, the Mormon leader, married his 27th, and last, wife in 1868.

- Even though the King James Bible was published in 1611, the Pilgrim Fathers carried the Geneva Bible with them to America in 1620. The King James Version had not become popular by then.

- According to Scottish novelist and politician John Buchan, 'An atheist is a man who has no invisible means of support.'

Sport and
Games

SPORT AND GAMES

- A rodeo cowboy has to stay on the bull for only eight seconds in a bull-riding contest – but few make it.

- The discus throw is the only track-and-field event for which a world record has never been set in Olympic competition.

- The par for the world's longest golf hole – the 909-yard (831-m) seventh hole on Japan's Sano golf course – is 7.

- Bowling was originally known in ancient Germany as *Heidenwerfen*, which means 'strike down the heathens'.

- Frank Sinatra had one thing in common with basketball star Kareem Abdul-Jabbar: they both weighed 13 lb (6 kg) at birth.

- Heavyweight boxing champion Ken Norton was rejected for the role of Apollo Creed in the 1976 film *Rocky* because he made star Sylvester Stallone look too small.

- In the original Olympics, trainers were required to attend in the nude. This was to stop women sneaking into the competitions, from which they were banned. One woman had attended an event disguised as her son's trainer. Thereafter the nude ruling was brought in.

—————— SPORT AND GAMES ——————

- In archery, when an arrow pierces another arrow, which is already in the bullseye, it is called a 'Robin Hood'.

- In horse racing a walkover is when a horse is uncontested in a race and simply has to walk the course to win.

- The only sport that takes place on a triangular racecourse is sailing.

- Boxing world champion Rocky Marciano nicknamed his deadly right hand 'Suzi-Q'.

- The first man to run the four-minute mile, England's Roger Bannister, held the world-record title for only 46 days. Australian John Landy knocked 1.4 seconds off his time on 21 June 1954.

- Horse racing has a sex allowance. Mares are permitted to carry 3 to 5 lb (1 to 2 kg) less weight when running against males in a thoroughbred horse race.

- The odds of getting four of a kind in a five-card deal in poker are 4,164 to 1.

- The maximum permitted weight of a shoe in a game of horseshoes is 2 ½ lb (1 kg).

SPORT AND GAMES

- King James II of Scotland banned golf in 1457 because, he said, it distracted the men from archery practice needed for national defence.

- The first tennis millionaire was Australian Rod Laver in 1971. He was twice Wimbledon Champion.

- The French boxing federation officially banned fighters from kissing one another at the end of their bouts in 1924.

- A bad shot that turns out well in golf is known as a Volkswagen in golfing slang.

- In 1956 the Physical Culture and Sports Commission of communist China recognised the sport of hand-grenade throwing.

- The Japanese company Nintendo made playing cards before it became involved in making computer games.

- When you hit a tennis ball it spends just $\frac{1}{1000}$ th of a second (0.004) in contact with the racquet.

- The very first video game, introduced in 1972, was Pong.

SPORT AND GAMES

- America's last professional bare-knuckle boxing bout, in 1889, went to 75 rounds. The fight was between John L Sullivan and Jake Kilrain – Kilrain lost. The famous lawman Bat Masterson was the timekeeper.

- The odds against a professional golf player scoring a hole-in-one are 15,000 to 1 against.

- Catgut, used in stringing tennis racquets, comes from the intestines of sheep, horses and several other animals – but definitely not the cat. It is possible the word was shortened from the original 'cattlegut'.

- Fourteen-year-old Nadia Comaneci of Romania was the first ever to receive a perfect '10' in an Olympic gymnastic competition. That was in 1976.

- Horses race clockwise in England and anti-clockwise in the United States.

- The game of ninepins, taken to America by the Dutch in the seventeenth century, was changed to tenpins in the 1840s. Because of heavy gambling on the game New York and Connecticut banned ninepin bowling. But since the ban did not apply to bowling in general, a tenth pin was added to get around the law.

SPORT AND GAMES

- Mohammed Ali's Citizens' Band (CB) name is Big Bopper.

- The colours blue, red, yellow, black and green were chosen for the Olympic rings because at least one of them appears on the flag of every nation in the world.

- The word 'furlong' in horse racing – a distance of an eighth of a mile (201 m) – dates from the days when a race was a furrow long, the length of a ploughed field.

- There were no rounds when boxing was introduced at the 23rd ancient Olympiad in 776 BC. Contestants fought until one man either dropped or gave in. There were no breaks.

- In the ancient Olympic Games archers used tethered doves as targets.

- Oscar Swahn, was the oldest person to win an Olympic medal. The Swede won a silver medal for shooting in 1920 when he was 72.

- The oldest driver in the 1979 Le Mans 24-hour endurance race was actor Paul Newman.

--------------- SPORT AND GAMES ---------------

- In cross-country bike racing the initials BMX stand for Bicycle Moto Cross (X).

- The International Skating Union recognises 48 different types of figure-of-eight.

- The heaviest heavyweight boxer to compete in a title fight was Italy's Primo Carnera, who weighed 19 stone 4 lb (270 lb or 122.5 kg) when he beat Tommy Loughran in 1934.

- The first woman to wear shorts at Wimbledon – on the centre court – was Lili de Alvarez in 1931.

- The odds against hitting the jackpot on the average slot machine are 889 to 1.

- There are over 600,000 million possible bridge hands that can be dealt from a pack of cards.

- The French dice game known as 'Hazard' was introduced into the United States – in New Orleans – in 1813, by a Creole. Creoles, because of their French associations, were sometimes nicknamed Johnny Crapauds, the word 'crapaud' being French for toad or frog. At first it was referred to as Crapaud's game, but was later shortened to 'Craps'.

--------------- **SPORT AND GAMES** ---------------

- During a 100 m race a top sprinter makes contact with the ground only some 40 times.

- The world's fastest racquet sport is badminton, where the shuttlecock reaches speeds of nearly 200 mph (322 kph).

- Germany is the country that in 1936 established the modern Olympic tradition of having the flame carried from Greece to the site of the games.

- King George VI competed at Wimbledon in 1926 when he was Duke of York. The left-hander lost his first-round doubles match.

- Jay Silverheels, otherwise known as Tonto of *Lone Ranger* fame, was once the highest-paid, highest-scoring lacrosse player in Canadian history.

- All five sons of heavyweight boxing champion George Foreman are called George.

- Zugzwang is a situation in chess when all possible moves are to a player's disadvantage.

- The standard pitching distance in a game of horseshoes is 40 ft (12 m) for men and 30 ft (9 m) for women.

SPORT AND GAMES

- The first driver to cover a mile in less than a minute in a petrol engine car was Barney Oldfield in 1903. He did a mile in 59.6 seconds driving a Ford 999.

- Jockeys are strapped to their mounts with Velcro during camel races in Abu Dhabi.

- Professional boxing gloves weigh 8 oz (approx. 224 g).

- The 'pone' is the person who sits on the dealer's right in a card game.

- The first Indianapolis 500 motor race in 1911 was won at an average speed of 74.59 mph (120 kph).

- The game of billiards gave us the word 'debut'. It is derived from the French word '*débuter*' which means 'to lead off'.

- The phrase 'turning point' comes from chariot racing. It was the place where a chariot driver turned at each end of the stadium.

- The fastest tennis serve ever recorded was that of Bill Tilden, in 1931, which was measured at 163.6 mph (263 kph).

SPORT AND GAMES

- A throw of five on the dice is known as a Little Phoebe in craps.

- Major league baseball bats are all made from ash.

FOOD

FOOD

- The largest apple pie ever baked was 40 x 23 ft (12 x 7 m).

- In America 69% of men and 57% of women drink beer.

- In Japan Christmas Eve is a time to eat strawberry shortcake and fried chicken.

- Tabasco sauce is made by fermenting vinegar with hot peppers in a French oak barrel, which has three inches of salt on top and is aged for three years until all the salt is defused through the barrel.

- After a coffee seed is planted it takes five years before the resulting plant can produce consumable fruit.

- At McDonald's in New Zealand they serve apricot pies instead of cherry ones.

- Reindeer milk has more fat than cow's milk.

- Tic-Tacs contain carnauba wax – the same ingredient found in many car polishes.

- After the Popeye cartoon started in 1931 spinach consumption in the United States went up by 33%.

FOOD

- The oldest recipe in existence is a recipe for beer.

- The ancient Romans often paid their taxes in honey.

- More cat food is bought in Britain each year than can be eaten by the number of cats in the country.

- Sarsaparilla is the root that flavours root beer.

- In Hong Kong soya milk is as popular as Coca-Cola is in the West.

- Pecans are the only food that astronauts do not have to treat and dehydrate when flying in space.

- A can of Spam is opened every four seconds.

- Almonds are members of the peach family.

- Butter was the first food product allowed to have artificial colouring by law. It is totally white in its natural state.

- You can make a glass of apple cider with only three apples.

- Cream does not weigh as much as milk.

---------------------------- FOOD ----------------------------

- An average person drinks between 10,000 and 12,000 gallons (45,460–54,552 litres) of water during their lifetime.

- Cranberries are sorted for ripeness by bouncing them. A ripe cranberry can be dribbled like a basketball.

- Germany has a beer ice cream in Popsicle form. Its alcohol content is lower than that of normal beer.

- Scientists in Denmark found that beer tastes best when drunk to the accompaniment of a certain musical tone. Apparently the optimum frequency is different for each beer, with the correct harmonious tone for drinking Carlsberg Lager being between 510 to 520 cycles per second.

- The Pilgrims ate popcorn during the first Thanksgiving dinner.

- More people are allergic to cow's milk than to any other food.

- Manufacturers of Old Grandad whisky produced their product throughout Prohibition by marking the bottles 'for medicinal purposes'.

FOOD

- You cannot taste food unless it is mixed with saliva. This is true for all foods.

- Beer was often served with breakfast in medieval England.

- French fries were invented in Belgium.

- Americans eat 12,000 million bananas each year.

- Turnips turn green when sunburned.

- You should not eat a crayfish with a straight tail. It means it was dead before it was cooked.

- The nutmeg tree produces two spices. Nutmeg is from the nut kernel itself and mace comes from the kernel's lacy covering.

- In 1867 Napoleon III commanded chemists to produce a special kind of food for the army and navy. It was margarine.

- The Muppet Miss Piggy said: 'Never eat more than you can lift.'

- Bombay duck is dry, salted fish.

FOOD

- It takes 75,000 crocus flowers to produce 1 lb (0.5 kg) of saffron – which is why it is the most expensive spice in the world.

- US President Kennedy's wife Jaqueline had the recipe for daiquiris pinned to the wall of the White House kitchen. It was the couple's favourite drink.

- In making bourbon whisky 51% of the grain that is used must be corn.

- The herring is the most widely eaten fish in the world.

- In Denmark Danish pastry is known as Vienna bread.

- Wild rice is not rice but a coarse annual grass that grows in shallow water or marshland.

- The peanut is a vegetable and a member of the pea family.

- Dr Miles's compound extract of tomato – an early ketchup – was sold as a medicine in the nineteenth century.

- Queen Victoria mixed her claret with whisky. The resulting brew was her favourite alcoholic drink.

FOOD

- Black-eyed peas are beans.

- The first commercially manufactured breakfast cereal was shredded wheat, made by Henry Perky in 1882.

- The pineapple originated in South America and did not reach Hawaii until the early nineteenth century.

- Pepper is the top-selling spice in the world. The second is mustard.

- In order for decaffeinated coffee to be so labelled it must have 97% of its caffeine removed, under American federal regulations.

- The coiffe is the metal wire basket that holds a champagne cork in place.

- Guests to multi-millionaire Alfred de Rothschild's mansion, in Buckinghamshire, England, who asked for milk in their tea were offered a choice between 'Hereford, Jersey or Shorthorn'!

- Pound cake received its name from the 1-lb quantities of the main ingredients – sugar, butter, eggs and flour – used in the original recipe.

—————————— FOOD ——————————

- The first name of blind cellar monk Dom Perignon, who discovered champagne, was Pierre.

- The father of the Gimlet cocktail was Sir T O Gimlette, a British naval surgeon who insisted his fellow officers drink gin and lime juice as he believed it to be healthier than drinking neat gin.

- Ancient Egyptians would place their right hands on an onion when swearing on oath. Its round shape symbolised eternity.

- There are no bananas in banana oil. It is a synthetic compound made with amyl-alcohol and gets its name simply from its banana-like aroma.

- The largest fruit crop on earth is grapes – followed by bananas.
- New Orleans, US, consumes more ketchup per capita than any other place on earth.

- Eighty-seven per cent of fully fat milk is water.

SEX

SEX

- Elvis Presley called his penis 'Little Elvis.'

- A recent survey revealed that 25% of Swedish women had had sex with more than 50 men.

- Americans spend more money each year at strip clubs than at all the theatres and classical concert halls in the country combined.

- Men are four times more likely to sleep in the nude than women are.

- The Ramses condom is named after the great pharaoh Ramses II, who fathered more than 160 children!

- In ancient Rome men found guilty of rape had their testicles crushed between two stones as a punishment.

- The word 'pornography' is from the Greek *pornographus*, meaning 'writing about prostitutes'.

- One in every 300 births in the United States occurs in a vehicle.

- Married women are physically and mentally less healthy than single women.

---- **SEX** ----

- Nudity in public was considered perfectly acceptable in ancient Greece, but it was declared indecent if a man revealed an erection.

- The average person spends two weeks of their life kissing.

- Prostitutes revealed in a recent survey that the sexual act they are most often asked to perform is fellatio.

- The sperm count of American men is down 30% on 30 years ago.

- Residents of the island of Lesbos are Lesbosians, not Lesbians. Lesbians are so called because the Greek poet Sappho was from Lesbos. Many of her poems expressed her love for women, giving rise to her association with female homosexuality.

- According to a Caribbean cruise line 58% of the passengers are unable to wait more than ten hours before making love. A lifeboat is the fourth most popular place on a ship to have sex. The whirlpool bath is ranked the first.

- The average sexually active woman has sex 83 times a year.

SEX

- A candle is the artificial device most frequently used by women during masturbation, according to a recent American survey.

- In ancient Greece and Rome dildos were made out of animal horn, ivory, gold, silver – or even glass.

- England first introduced sex education in schools in 1889.

- Sixteen years and two months is the average age for the loss of female virginity in the United States.

- Placing a red light outside a brothel to advertise its wares was first introduced in 1234 in Avignon, France.

- More than one million condoms are sold each day in the United States – that being only 0.4% of the population.

- It is against the law to have sex on a parked motor cycle in London.

- Forty-six per cent of women say a good night's sleep is better than sex.

- Most exhibitionists are married men.

SEX

- Eleven per cent of women and 5% of men claim never to have masturbated.

- Menstrual cramps have been known, in rare cases, to induce orgasm.

- The average bra size is now 36C. Ten years ago it was 34B.

- Seventy-one per cent of women between the ages of eighteen and twenty are at ease being seen nude by their lover; 51% of men are at ease being seen nude by their girlfriend.

- Today there is a 75% chance that a TV programme during family viewing time will contain sexually related talk or behaviour.

- Most American women say they would rather receive chocolate than flowers on St Valentine's Day.

- Humans spend two years of their lives making love.

- Only 31% of men admit to looking at other woman when in the company of their spouse or girlfriend. Their partners say this figure is actually 64%.

SEX

- On average it takes two tablespoons of blood to make a man's penis erect.

- Seventy per cent of Swedish women claim to have participated in a threesome.

- Every year more than 11,000 Americans hurt themselves trying out bizarre sexual positions.

- Sex burns off 360 calories an hour.

- America's first manufactured condoms appeared in 1870 and were made of vulcanised rubber. They were thick, insensitive and intended to be reused.

- A winged penis was the city symbol of Pompeii, the ancient Roman resort town destroyed by the eruption of Mount Vesuvius.

- Homosexuality was still on the American Psychiatric Association's list of mental illnesses until 1973.

- The average penguin has only one orgasm a year.

- Less than 30% of parents say they can openly discuss sex with their children.

---------- SEX ----------

- A real orgasm is said to burn 112 calories. A fake orgasm is said to burn off 315 calories.

- The heart beats faster during a brisk walk or a good argument than it does during sexual intercourse.

- Four popes died while participating in sexual acts.

STATISTICS

--- **STATISTICS** ---

- Sixty-seven per cent of dog owners buy holiday gifts for their pet.

- Every day 240,000 pairs of Pretty Polly tights are made in Sutton-in-Ashfield in Nottinghamshire, UK.

- Sixty per cent of British women believe their legs to be about average.

- Thirty per cent of British women think their legs are poor.

- One per cent of British women think their legs are perfect.

- Thirty-nine per cent of women who think their legs are fat still wear short skirts.

- The dead outnumber the living on earth by about 25 to 1.

- The Battle of Waterloo lasted nine and a half hours.

- The average number of alcoholic drinks consumed by male marathon runners in a week is fourteen.

- The odds of being in a plane crash are 1 in 750,000.

STATISTICS

- Twelve per cent of the British population are left-handed.

- Ninety-seven per cent of Canadians would not borrow a toothbrush if they forgot to pack their own.

- If you had enough water to fill one million goldfish bowls you could fill an entire stadium.

- Forty-four per cent of all adults are estimated to go on a diet at least once a year.

- Only 55% of Americans know that the sun is a star.

- About 30,000 Americans are injured by toilets every year.

- The average person has more than 1,460 dreams a year.

- At least 35% of adults are 20% or more above their recommended weight.

- If you gave every human on earth their own piece of land then, counting uninhabitable areas, each one would get 100 square feet.

- The average person laughs thirteen times a day.

STATISTICS

- The average person over 50 will have spent a year looking for lost or mislaid items.

- Seventy-eight per cent of pets never travel with their owners.

- Forty-five per cent of cat owners buy a holiday gift for their pet.

- Eighty-three per cent of people hit by lightning are men.

- Ten per cent of men do not care what their partners' legs look like.

- Meteorologists claim they are right 85% of the time.

- Ninety per cent of bird species are monogamous.

- Fifty per cent of Western women say they would marry the same man again; 80% of men say they would marry the same woman again.

- Fifty-eight per cent of men say they are happier after their divorce or separation.

- There is a lawsuit every 30 seconds in the United States.

STATISTICS

- Eighty-five per cent of women say they are happier after their divorce or separation.

- It has been calculated that in the last 3,500 years there have only been 230 years of peace in the civilised world.

- Forty per cent of women admit to having thrown footwear at men.

- The chances of being killed by falling out of bed are less than one in two million.

- The odds of being hit by space debris are one in five billion.

- In 75% of American households the women manage the money and pay the bills.

- Right-handed people live, on average, nine years longer than left-handed people.

- On average, each year 55,700 people are injured by jewellery.

- Driving at 55 mph (89 kph) instead of 65 mph (105 kph) increases your car mileage by about 15%.

STATISTICS

- The average iceberg weighs twenty million tons.

- A four-year-old child asks an average of 437 questions a day.

- Six per cent of American men say they proposed to their wives on the phone.

- Forty-eight per cent of people say that Santa Claus and gift-giving detract from the religious celebration of Christmas.

- Sixty-eight per cent of teenage girls would choose their stomach if they were allowed to change one part of their body.

- Forty-four per cent of people say they spend too much at Christmas.

- Twenty-two per cent of men leave their Christmas shopping until the last two days before Christmas Day. Only 9% of women do the same.

- The average human produces 50,000 pints (28,400 litres) of spit in a lifetime – the equivalent of two small swimming pools.

STATISTICS

- Ninety per cent of Irish women are unhappy with their legs.

- Forty per cent of Scottish women have legs that are different lengths.

- The average person in America spends eight years of their lives watching television.

- If we had the same mortality rate now that we had in the year 1900, more than half the people in the world today would not be alive.

- Twelve per cent of people start their Christmas shopping with the January sales.

- If the population of China began walking past you in single file, the line would never end because of the rate of reproduction.

- Eighty-five per cent of men do not use the front opening of their underpants when they urinate.

Last Words

—————— LAST WORDS ——————

- 'This is no time to be making new enemies.'
    Voltaire, in reply to the Bishop of Paris when asked on his deathbed to renounce the devil and turn to God.

- 'The earth is suffocating. Swear to make them cut me open, so I won't be buried alive.'
    Frederic Chopin

- 'I'm sorry to disappoint the vultures.'
    Stephen Ward, Profumo-scandal scapegoat

- 'I've had eighteen straight whiskies – I think that's a record. After 39 years this is all I've done.'
    Dylan Thomas

- 'Tell me, Gene, is it true you're the illegitimate son of Buffalo Bill Cody?'
    Actor John Barrymore, speaking to a deathbed friend

- 'I realise that patriotism is not enough. I must have no hatred or bitterness towards anyone.'
    Edith Cavell, the British nurse executed as a spy

- 'If I say goodnight to you now, will you promise that I won't wake up again?'
    Film producer Alexander Korda

LAST WORDS

- 'I think I could eat one of Bellamy's veal pies.'
  Prime Minister Pitt the Younger

- 'Dammit. Put them back on. This is funny.'
  Gunfighter 'Doc' Holliday, after his boots were removed

- 'You can do that more easily to my dead body.
  Come, be quick!'
  *Louis Philippe, Duke of Orleans, speaking
  to the executioner removing his boots*

- 'The bullet hasn't been made that can kill me.'
  Gangster 'Legs' Diamond

- 'Get my "swan" costume ready.'
  Russian ballerina Anna Pavlova

- 'Drink to me.'
  Pablo Picasso

- 'I can't sleep.'
  Peter Pan author James Barrie

- 'It would really be more than the English could stand if
  another century began and I were still alive. I am dying
  as I have lived – beyond my means.'
  Oscar Wilde

—————— LAST WORDS ——————

- 'Be natural, my children. For the writer that is natural
  has fulfilled all the rules of art.'

  Charles Dickens

- 'Take away those pillows – I shall need them no more.'

  Lewis Carroll (Charles Lutwidge Dodgson)

- 'What is the noise?'
  Daughter: 'It's the people outside.'
  'What are they doing?'
  Daughter: 'They've come to say "Goodbye".'
  'Why? Where are they going?'

  Dictator Generalissimo Franco

- 'Nothing but death.'

  Jane Austen, when asked if she wanted anything

- 'Death, the only immortal, who treats us all alike, whose
  peace and whose refuge are for all. The soiled and the
  pure, the rich and the poor, the loved and the unloved.'

  Mark Twain

- 'If I feel in good form I shall take the difficult way up. If
  I do not, I shall take the easy way up. I shall join you in
  an hour.'

  King Alfred I of Belgium, killed mountain climbing

—— LAST WORDS ——

- 'Prithee, let me feel the axe. I fear it is not sharp enough. Do not hack me as you did my Lord Russell.'

  James, Duke of Monmouth, beheaded

- 'Oh God, here I go!'

  Heavyweight boxer Max Baer

- 'Can this last long?'

  King William III

- 'In the name of modesty, cover my bosom.'

  Elizabeth, sister of King Louis XVI, guillotined

- 'I am always angry when I'm dying.'

  Clifford Mortimer, barrister father of John

- 'Goodnight, my darlings, I'll see you tomorrow.'

  Noel Coward

- 'I've never felt better.'

  Actor Douglas Fairbanks Sr

- 'Do you know where the apothecary lives? Then send and let him know that I would like to see him. I don't feel quite well and I will lie still until he comes.'

  Duke of Wellington

———— LAST WORDS ————

- 'Sister, you're trying to keep me alive as an old curiosity. But I'm done. I am finished. I'm going to die.'

  George Bernard Shaw

- 'Well I've played everything but a harp.'

  Lionel Barrymore

- 'I desire to go to hell and not to heaven. In the former place I will enjoy the company of popes, kings and princes, while in the latter only beggars, monks and apostles.'

  Niccolò Machiavelli

- 'That was the best ice-cream soda I ever tasted.'

  US comedian Lou Costello

- 'See that Yul (Brynner) gets star billing. He has earned it.'

  Gertrude Lawrence, star of the film The King and I

- 'If you would send for a doctor I will see him now.'

  Emily Brontë

- 'Now I want to go home. Don't weep. What I have done is best for all of us. No use. I shall never get rid of this depression.'

  Vincent van Gogh

—— LAST WORDS ——

- 'I guess you were right, Wyatt. I can't see a damn thing.'
  Police officer Morgan Earp, speaking to his brother,
  Wyatt, who denied afterlife existed

- 'I should never have switched from Scotch to Martinis.'
  Humphrey Bogart

- 'This is it. I'm going. I'm going.'
  Al Jolson, Russian-born American singer,
  film actor and comedian

- 'I'm going. Perhaps it is for the best.'
  US President John Tyler

- 'This is my final word. It is time for me to become an apprentice once more. I have not settled in which direction. But somewhere. Sometime. Soon.'
  Lord Beaverbrook, British Conservative politician
  and newspaper proprietor

- 'There is no one in the kingdom that will make me his master. My time has come to die.'
  Confucius

- 'On the whole, I would rather be in Philadelphia.'
  W C Fields

LAST WORDS

- 'I do not know which is more difficult in a Christian life
  – to live well or to die well.'

  Daniel Defoe

- 'May I please have a cigar?'

  John Ford, film director

- 'I think it's time for morphine.'

  D H Lawrence

- 'Please put out the light.'

  US President Theodore Roosevelt

- 'The executioner is, I believe, an expert and my neck is
  very slender. Oh God, have pity on my soul.'

  Anne Boleyn

- 'I can't feel anything in my right leg. I can't feel anything
  in my left leg. Doctor, are my eyes open? I can't see.'

  'Manolete', matador

- 'I always was beautiful.'

  Pauline Bonaparte, Napoleon's sister

- 'What is the scaffold? A short-cut to heaven.'

  Charles Peace, hanged killer

——— LAST WORDS ———

- 'I have offended God and mankind because my work did not reach the quality it should have.'

  Leonardo da Vinci

- 'Excuse my dust.'

  Dorothy Parker, wit

- 'Now I know that I must be very ill, as you have been sent for.'

  Henry Longfellow, poet

- 'My fun days are over.'

  James Dean

- 'Remember me to my friends. Tell them I'm a hell of a mess.'

  H L Mencken, journalist

- 'What matter how the head lie, so the heart be right? 'Tis a sharp remedy, but a sure one for all ills.'

  Sir Walter Raleigh, when told his head lay the wrong way for beheading

- 'He makes a very nice corpse, and becomes his coffin prodigiously.'

  Oliver Goldsmith, Irish novelist, poet, essayist and dramatist

LAST WORDS

- 'A king should die standing up.'

  Louis XVIII of France, trying to rise

- 'That was a great game of golf.'

  Bing Crosby

- 'Go away. I'm all right.'

  H G Wells

- 'God bless. Goddamn!'

  James Thurber, cartoonist

- 'Better not. She would only ask me to take a message to Albert.'

  Prime Minister Benjamin Disraeli, asked if he wished to see Queen Victoria at his deathbed

- 'If this is dying, then I don't think much of it.'

  Lytton Strachey, English author

END QUOTES

———— END QUOTES ————

- 'Death is the most convenient time to tax rich people.'

  Prime Minister David Lloyd George

- 'Once you're dead, you're made for life.'

  Jimi Hendrix

- 'Either he's dead or my watch has stopped.'

  Groucho Marx

- 'He makes a very nice corpse, and becomes his coffin prodigiously.'

  Oliver Goldsmith, Irish novelist, poet, essayist and dramatist

- 'It's not that I'm afraid to die. I just don't want to be there when it happens.'

  Woody Allen